Finding Home in God's Heart

Recovering
From a
Dysfunctional
Family Background

Tim Rule
FOUNDER OF InnerLife Ministries

Finding Home in God's Heart
Recovering From a Dysfunctional Family Background
By Tim Rule
InnerLife Ministries © 2021

All Bible verses are from the English Standard Version (ESV) unless otherwise stated.

Cover and Interior Design: Fusion Creative Works, FusionCW.com
Lead Editor: Megan Terry

ISBN: 978-1-7377273-0-9

Printed in the United States of America

Contents

Introduction

People are not shaped in a vacuum. How you think; and what you believe; how you view yourself, love, trust, forgiveness, marriage, and what a father and mother is—all of this has been highly influenced by culture and primarily by your family of origin.

Imagine if a baby was able to be put into a spaceship, equipped to meet all of their physical needs for up to 20 years, and was launched into space, cast away from the earth for the first 20 years of their life, with no contact. Would that child, who eventually would become a fully grown person physically, have any idea of who they were and what life is about? The answer I would give is a resounding no. They would have no reference point to understand themselves. We developed an understanding of ourselves through an accumulation of thousands of interactions with others throughout our growing years, through verbal and nonverbal communication. However, the most life-impacting voices are family members.

Your family of origin greatly influences how you see yourself. We each have a mental picture, a personal assessment, of our character, personality, sexuality, skills, abilities, and other attributes that was greatly influenced by our family backgrounds. It's from this personal assessment—however positive or negative, rational or irrational— that we determine how we present ourselves to others.

Our family environments and the culture in which we operate can generate tremendous amounts of pain and stress that can devastate our inner lives. We struggle with personal baggage for good reason. Contrary to what was intended, I believe most of the environments we live in are toxic, anxiety- and pain-producing environments.

Because of these dynamics, we are in great need of sorting out our inner lives and discovering what true spiritual, emotional, and relational health is. That is the need this book serves.

The content of this book is designed to help people unearth and identify their "default beliefs" that have led to problems like disconnection, frustration, broken and strained relationships, pain, hopelessness, and so many other life hurts we experience.

You will learn how your family of origin has shaped you, explore your default beliefs about life and relationships, and process why all of this matters. You will learn to understand the negative impact of the family environments many of us were raised in, and how the root causes of our family backgrounds have led many people to feel so unhappy.

It's my intention to help you get "under the hood," to understand your heart and increase your awareness of the central issues underlying your particular personal struggles. It is my prayer that working through and processing the content of this book will lead to an inner life characterized by real joy, love, hope, and peace. It is also my great hope that this book's contents will help you generate great amounts of understanding and compassion for yourself and for others who come from hurting homes.

The majority of the content in this book has come from working through my own inner life and relational issues. I've come a long way from the man I was, but I have plenty more I still need to work on. This book is also the result of over 35 years of research and experience coming alongside others to help sort through their inner life and relational issues. I'm told I'm a gifted counselor and naturally talented in these areas, but that will be for you to determine after reading this content. Most importantly, I've had the deep pleasure and privilege to sit under some of the greatest theologians and thought leaders in these subjects from around the country. This book is an accumulation of the wisdom and insights that I've gained from multiple mentors through the years. Words cannot fully express how grateful I am for their investment in my life.

It's important to understand the foundational presupposition of this book: I'm writing this from a God-centered, Biblical perspective. If you come from a Christian background, you may immediately understand and be familiar with many of the subjects I discuss. You may also be surprised at some new discoveries you make. If you do not have a Christian background, I believe you will still find valuable, life giving, helpful perspectives that will make this well worth your time.

It's my hope you will discover how God practically and effectively helps us address our hearts and inner lives and that you will find opportunities to wrestle with your default beliefs. God's heart is to help you identify and address false beliefs and encourage new belief patterns.

If you are looking for a quick fix to your issues, this book will likely be a disappointment. There are no quick fixes! I am not—and I believe God is not—offering you a silver bullet to your complex inner life and relational problems. I am offering gospel-centered perspectives, concepts, and truths that will help you on your journey toward a more joyful and peaceful heart. But make no mistake about it, it's going to take time, effort, intentionality, mindfulness, and people near you to support you along the way.

Thousands of people have now gone through my workbook and process called *Untying the Knots of the Heart* (much of the same content in this book can be found in the *UTK* workbook) and have been transformed by these perspectives and concepts. I believe it can greatly help your journey toward more joy, peace, love, and hope as well.

> If practiced, these truths, perspectives, and concepts, grounded in the deep love of God the Father, will greatly reduce and reframe many inner-life issues with which you may be struggling.

You may be reading these statements with a good deal of doubt and skepticism. You may believe it's not possible to overcome your inner-life issues or even reduce the symptoms you are feeling. You may feel your pain and struggles are too powerful. Perhaps you are a Christian, and your Bible reading and Christianity, up to this point, seem not to have helped reduce your anxiety, depression, anger, or other problems at all. As a matter of fact, those practices may have even increased the pain and frustration.

I invite you to bring all your honesty, fears, and skepticism, as well as all your heart to every chapter of this book. It is my hope that by the end of the book your doubts will be replaced with a rich, confident relationship and trust in God. To get to the bottom of our pain, doubts, and fears, we each need to do some exploration. I strongly believe this exploration is best done within the context of safe friends.

Effectively addressing your inner life issues is best accomplished by talking about them with others. It is only when we talk with God and others about what we're thinking, what we're believing, what we're feeling, and what our desires are that we can more clearly see, think through, and sort out our inner-life issues. Spiritual and emotional healing happens when we process our hearts with other people. It's a powerful thing when you're talking about your struggles with someone and you see them nod their heads in understanding and agreement. It can make us feel less alone. Watching others lean toward us and accept us while talking about our struggles can make us feel valued and comforted.

It helps us to say out loud what's going on in our heads. It helps to explain to someone else, even when it doesn't make any sense, what you're feeling and thinking. Why? Because as you try to organize your thoughts to explain them to others, it can bring clarity to you as well as to those listening, most of whom are likely thinking and feeling the same way. Talking to others leads to catharsis. Catharsis is a feeling of awareness and relief. Processing your fears and anxieties with others tends to drain off much of the pain and overwhelming emotion. When you open your mouth and heart, knowing that others are truly hearing you, you can begin to feel understood—which is soothing to the soul.

Sharing our experiences with others helps us to get out of our self-defeating patterns. In the introduction to his autobiographical memoir, *The Sacred Journey*, Frederick Buechner writes, "My assumption is that the story of any one of us is in some measure the story of all of us." When we choose to bury our feelings, thoughts, and life experiences from others, it not only isolates us, but it also serves to isolate others as well. When we express how we really feel and what we're really thinking (in an appropriate manner), we begin to figure things out, solve problems, mend relationships, and make better sense of life.

I highly encourage you to use this book in the context of a small-group environment to help people effectively process their family backgrounds with others. What a gift it would be to give others the time, a safe place, and an intentional process to contemplate the effects of their family backgrounds through the loving eyes of a compassionate God.

If you want to experience true love, connectedness, joy, and peace, it will require you to be real with others. Being real requires vulnerability. For most of us who have been hurt by others, vulnerability seems like a really bad idea! It's possible that vulnerability was what led you to become so hurt and anxious. This may seem counterintuitive, but vulnerability is the first step toward healing.

We were made for connection and rich relationships. That's what man was meant to experience in a garden with God and with one another. We were designed to thrive in an environment of trust, love, and unashamed joy. Then it all fell apart in the garden (Genesis 1-3). The consequences of Adam and Eve's decision left scars on all humankind. We are now immersed in a chaotic, pain-filled world. From a Biblical point of view, we swim in a relatively toxic environment that massively impacts our physical, emotional, relational, and spiritual health. Not only is our physical environment filled with pain and fear, but mankind's relational environment—with God and each other—brims with toxic levels of shame, guilt, worthlessness, broken trusts, unaddressed or mismanaged pain, fear, anger, hopelessness, and loss of every kind.

As followers of Christ, we need to embrace the reality of our brokenness. It gives us the freedom to be real and vulnerable with others. According to the Bible, *all* have sinned and fallen short of the glory of God (Romans 3:23). With confidence, we can look each other in the eye and say, "I've got problems. I struggle, and so do you." Each one of us struggles with inner-life issues. Everyone experiences relational problems. You can be real with others about your problems because we all have problems. It's okay to say, "I'm not okay."

The Bible tells us to take off our "old self" (Colossians 3:9-10). But how can you take off something you have not clearly identified? To do this, it is critically important for each of us to gain a firm understanding of the forces that have shaped our instincts and default beliefs, both positively and negatively.

As you read, you may be triggered by certain words in this book—words like abuse, neglect, dysfunction, victims, and victimizers. Reading these words or words like these, you may think or feel, "That's not me. I don't need a book like this; my family wasn't that bad." And that very well could be the case. Statistically speaking though, it is likely that you come from a dysfunctional family or are in one now. Like many of us, you may have never slowed down enough and asked the right questions to discover exactly how healthy your family's relational environment was or is, and what impact it has had on your life. Whatever the case may be, I want to encourage you to keep reading, at least to understand what many of your friends, relatives, coworkers, and neighbors are experiencing, and why they do what they do. More importantly, I would like you to learn how God can make a profound difference in their lives, and how they can recover from their family backgrounds.

Once we've examined our default beliefs, I will begin the process of introducing you to the family environment of the Trinity. We will explore the environment God intends us to experience with Him. God's true family environment should shape our default beliefs about ourselves, others, and Him far more deeply than those of our fallen world.

At the end of each chapter, you will find questions to aid you in understanding and processing your own journey. If you are using this book in a small group, participants will find the questions helpful to discuss each chapter and process their family backgrounds with others.

We'll explore questions like these:

- What is a dysfunctional family?

- What are the effects of a dysfunctional family on your inner life and relationships?

- Was your home of origin dysfunctional?

- What are the unique dangers of a religiously confused home?

- What is a healthy family?

- How does God help us recover from a dysfunctional home?

The Lord has healing for you. He is on a search and rescue mission for each one of us, and his rescue is not just for heaven later. His rescue is also for the here-and-now, day-to-day, up-and-down, life-and-death moments of love and loss on this side of heaven. There are healthy, life-giving ways to move forward. These ways include understanding your family background; identifying the lies, false perceptions, and life perspectives that are influencing you at a deep level; and helping you see yourself and others through the eyes of a compassionate, loving, grace-filled Heavenly Father. He is for you, he cares deeply about you, and he delights in you. He is with us. Please join me in the journey toward our true home in God's heart.

CHAPTER 1

Why Look Back?

As described in the introduction, we are not shaped in a vacuum. Undoubtedly our childhood experiences and the influences of family are among the most powerful forces that shape us.

There are several reasons we need to examine our family backgrounds.

- Many, if not most, of our current issues stem from family background.

- Misguided views of God and our new, Heavenly Family are strongly influenced by family background.

- We may not even realize it, but many of us have built walls around ourselves because of wounds from our pasts. For some, their pasts were so painful, they have completely re-written their memories. Others choose to explain away the effects of abuse or neglect by saying, "My family did the best they could and no one meant to hurt me." Some may reason that it made them tough, strong, independent, and street-wise. While these may be true, it does not lessen the effects our pasts have on our hearts and on our ability to connect with and trust God and others.

As you examine your family background, you can better identify what issues do and do not come from your family environment so you can deal with them accordingly.

We all long for stable, safe, committed, joyful home environments, but they are hard to come by. Over half of today's marriages end in divorce. Over half of the children born in the U.S. are born to unwed mothers. Family dissolution is a fact of life. These statistics are true of individuals both inside and outside the church. (Hymowitz, et al, 2013)

An alarming number of people are growing up in abusive families or situations where physical and/or sexual abuse occurs. And emotional abuse and neglect are equally damaging and equally rampant, though not always as easy to observe and address.

Statistically, most Americans come from a dysfunctional family. (Bradshaw, 2010) Even beyond statistics, according to the Bible, no matter who our parents, siblings, friends, and family are, we all have a lethal, life-debilitating problem: sin.

The consequences of painful family environments leave their impressions on us. Issues of codependence, chemical dependence, addictions, depression, anxiety disorders, and inappropriate boundaries are just a handful of the conditions that can stem from this type of stress and pain-filled home environment.

When we slow down and honestly reflect on our lives, we often discover that our personal baggage—collected through years of swimming in a fallen world—affects our instinctual responses to stress and pain and our views of God and ourselves far more than God's words through the Bible affect us. Even those from fairly healthy families and those who have avoided many of our cultural pitfalls are not immune to the effects of mankind's fall and the sin pervading each human soul. Our fears and beliefs often lead us into behaviors we know are wrong, but we feel like we can't stop those behaviors. The stress and wounds of daily life seem to somehow trump the life-changing power of the gospel, robbing our inner peace and diminishing or even eliminating the healthy outcomes the Bible claims will be produced in us (love, joy, peace, patience, kindness, goodness, self- control, etc.).

Even though mankind collectively has done a good job of messing things up, God's intention is to rescue us from our fallen backgrounds. For men and women to recover from their fallen backgrounds, they have to be met by a greater life-changing force. Thus the need for us to hear from God.

A PICTURE HAS BEEN PAINTED ACROSS YOUR HEART

You carry a mental picture of yourself—your identity, who you believe you are—on both a conscious and subconscious level. This mental picture determines how and with whom you choose to interact on any given day. Your life goals are developed and influenced by your view of who you are, including who you want to be and who you try to avoid being.

"Self-identity" is a misnomer. People are not born with "self-identity." Rather, identity evolves over time. Young children have simple identities and see themselves in a basic, uncomplicated manner. As they grow older, they begin identifying themselves based on interactions with other people, and their responses grow in increasingly sophisticated ways.

Your identity comes from an accumulation of scripts or pictures you have been given, consciously and subconsciously, and have learned well throughout your life; it's been developed by thousands upon thousands of interactions, both verbal and nonverbal, with those around you. Most of these ideas come from key people and role models in your life. As you might imagine, your identity was shaped primarily between the ages of 2 and 18, and has been most influenced by your relationships with family, relatives, and peers.

Growing up, most of us experienced some mix of helpful voices and interactions, as well as damaging ones. Sorting out the voices in your head is critical to your ability to step toward spiritual, emotional, and relational health. You must sort out and see what was communicated to you: the words that were spoken or not spoken to you, and the actions that were taken or not taken toward you, that left wounds that have yet to heal, and voids that have yet to be filled.

You may feel some despair thinking about looking at your family background and its effects on you. "Why do I need to revisit the pains of my growing up years? I have tried so hard to forget all that! Aren't I supposed to just forget about my painful past?" It is not a pleasant experience to revisit wounds from our past, but it is critically important that we do.

God wants to bring true healing to your deepest hurt and inner pain. For that to happen, you must gain his mature and wise perspective on those hurtful events. I believe God is not a surface healer. To use an old adage, he doesn't put band-aids on bullet wounds. True forgiveness and peace come from understanding your past from God's perspective.

When we gain his perspective on relationships and events that deeply wounded us, we can put our hands to the plow and not look back (Luke 9:62). To change unhealthy behaviors and relational styles we have practiced since childhood, though, we must go back and understand where they came from and why we're entrenched in them. Many of us practice compulsive, unhealthy behaviors and are absolutely clueless about their effects. Why? Because those patterns and tendencies were simply part of life for us as we grew up. It's in revisiting the roots of these behaviors and tendencies from a mature, healthy perspective that we can finally understand them enough to change.

In looking back, it's important to feel briefly what you felt during the events of your childhood. I want you to just stick your toe in those emotions—don't soak in them. You need to experience the emotional and relational environment that so powerfully shaped you. Many of your instinctual responses to life come out of those critical years and the emotions you were feeling during them. But this time, as those memories come, you'll hold the hand of God the Father, who can give you what you really needed during that time—perspective and comfort. It was in your emotional response to events that forged you and your belief system that you developed a picture of yourself that was inaccurate at best and life-debilitating at worst.

A picture of yourself has been developed in your heart. This picture created through the years has communicated who you are and what you are worth. That self-picture highly influences how we relate to others, to our own hearts, and to God. The picture your family painted across your heart can be a positive legacy or it can be a painful curse.

There is a great need for us to better understand the family environment's impact on us. In the coming chapters, we will explore how brokenness happens in families and the most common effects on our inner lives and relationships.

What often goes unrecognized is how your family background affects your view of God. Your instincts of what a father is like affect your view of God. We'll ask honest questions like these: Did God know and care about what my family suffered or what I suffered? If so, why didn't he stop it?

It is important to sort through your family background; it has had a massive influence on your inner life and relationships, your view of self, and your view of God. I want to give you the gifts of time, perspectives, and biblical truths to help you sort out your family background. It is my prayer that you will discover God's great love and compassion for you and what you have experienced.

QUESTIONS

Do you believe that a person's family background can affect his or her view of God? If so how?

_____

_____

_____

_____

Do you have a need to sort through your family of origin?

_____

_____

_____

_____

In your own words, what would be the benefits of sorting out wounds from your past?

_____

_____

_____

_____

_____

What are you hoping to get out of this book?

_____

_____

_____

_____

CHAPTER 2

Understanding the Hurting Home

Growing up on our rural family property, my brothers and I were introduced early in our lives to the family business of steel fabrication. I saw and participated firsthand in the processes of cutting, bending, and shaping steel, forming the metal into specific shapes and sizes. Metal is heated to thousands of degrees and the liquid metal is poured. While still red-hot, the metal is easily moldable. But once it cools, it takes the hardened shape of the cast into which it has been poured.

The family has a similar effect on people. A child is like molten steel, being poured into the cast of the family environment. His or her concept of self, what love is, how relationships work, and how life works are deeply cast into the child's psyche.

God's family—the Trinity—is the only completely healthy family. The characteristics of God's family are the ones we were meant to know well and on which we were meant to build our lives. The challenge of introducing believers into God's family is that the only model they have to look to is the human family they have already experienced. Most of us would consider only a small percentage of families to be truly healthy.

The Bible tells us that the real number of healthy families is even smaller:

> What then? Are we better than they? Not at all; for we have already charged that both Jews and Greeks are all under sin; as it is written, "There is none righteous, not even one; there is none who understands, there is none who seeks for God; all have turned aside, together they have become useless. There is none who does good, there is not even one."
>
> "Their throat is an open grave, with their tongues they keep deceiving,"
>
> "The poison of asps is under their lips;"
>
> "Whose mouth is full of cursing and bitterness;"
>
> "Their feet are swift to shed blood, destruction and misery are in their paths, and the path of peace they have not known."
>
> "There is no fear of God before their eyes."
>
> —Romans 3:9-18 (NASB 1995)

"Together they have become useless." This describes all of us after the fall. Together, we are all dysfunctional and unhealthy.

God puts statistics for imperfect families at 100 percent. We feel relief when we finally "walk in the light," admitting pain and brokenness are part of ourselves, our families, and our world. But we are not without hope; now we can seek God to address the worthlessness we could not address ourselves.

"Walk in the light" comes from the Bible passage 1 John 1:3-2:2. It is important to note what this passage means by "God is light." In the minds of ancient people, "God is light" was not taken to mean God is a light source, like a light bulb or a sun. People knew John meant that God's nature, like light, is to reveal things that are hidden. His nature is to acknowledge and reveal to us what is true. In essence, John meant that if you walk in the light (not hiding or withholding yourself), you have something in common with God. If you walk in the light of what is true about you, you have something deeply in common with God the Father: you and God both see the truth of God's nature and your own condition.

Don't underestimate the effects of the family. Its pressures mold our inner lives into what we are today. Healthy or unhealthy, this tremendously powerful force, applied over a long period of time, conforms us to expectations of family life and relationships.

It's amazing how most of us grow up believing our own family backgrounds were normal. Usually, it's not until we interact with others as adults that we discover our family backgrounds may not have been that healthy. Many families seem normal at first glance. But when we scratch just below the surface, we usually find surprising amounts of dysfunction. The relationships between spouses, parents, and children are strained. Although there may be many different causes, the majority of families are stressed. Typically, one or more family members have some type of emotional or relational issue that impacts every other family member.

The majority of us were raised in hurting or dysfunctional homes, homes where parents or caregivers somehow did not adequately provide for their children's spiritual, mental, emotional, relational, or physical needs. Many of us come from homes where we experienced trauma from our parents' actions, words, attitudes, or lifestyles. We didn't realize we were missing necessary emotional and relational skills and perspectives that prepare us for adulthood.

For many of us, these experiences have led to attempting to flee the pain of our pasts through alcohol or drug use, sexual addictions, workaholism, or some other type of preoccupation. Some of us feel inexplicably compelled to repeat the very abuses that harmed us, inflicting them on our own children, spouses, friends, or coworkers. We live with inner anxiety or rage, and don't know why we feel the way we do. Often, we compulsively want to control everything and everyone in our lives. Many of us suffer from low self-esteem and wrestle with our own value and worth all our lives.

Needless to say, these traumas impact every aspect of life, from jobs to marriages to parenting. We are shut down emotionally. We mismanage our pain. We don't have the basic skills and perspectives to deal with relational problems.

WHAT IS A DYSFUNCTIONAL HOME?

Let me begin by first defining what a dysfunctional home is and its implications.

A dysfunctional home is created when caregivers subject children to abnormal emotional, physical, and/or relational pain and stress due to neglect, abandonment, or abuse. To cope, the children learn to use instinctive, childlike strategies to protect themselves. As these children grow and enter adult relationships, they instinctively approach life's pain and stress with the same unaddressed childlike beliefs, perspectives, and strategies they formed as children, thus perpetuating the dysfunctional cycle.

When a child is immersed into a home environment that has abnormal amounts of ongoing stress and pain, it's likely they are part of a dysfunctional family, especially if the child is subjected to stress and pain from parents or caregivers struggling with alcoholism, drugs, and/or abuse and emotional neglect. Children raised in these types of hurting homes typically suffer extensive, lingering effects.

All children experience some degree of pain and stress while growing up. Some level of pain and stress is normal and a simple reality of life in a fallen world.

Here are a few examples of **normal stress**:

- Being sick

- Feeling too hot or too cold

- Being injured

- Losing pets or loved ones

- The first day of school

- Making new friends

These are regular life stresses, not dysfunctional family stresses. Most every child in the world experiences these.

However, it's critical to understand *abnormal stress*, which differentiates a healthy home from a dysfunctional home environment.

Here are some examples of **abnormal stress**:

- A child or adolescent having to be a parent to their parent(s)

- Worrying about being hit or beaten by a caregiver

- Being sexually molested

- Continually wondering if they are acceptable to their parent(s) or caregiver(s)

- The unpredictability created by drug or alcohol addiction in a home

- Being physically or emotionally abandoned or neglected

- Not being able to talk about life's daily problems with parent(s) or caregiver(s)

- Lack of closure and resolution of a traumatic family event

- Lack of healthy affection/affirmation, creating the stress of trying to earn approval

THE EFFECTS OF PHYSICAL, SEXUAL, AND EMOTIONAL ABUSE

Common sense says that a parent or caregiver should do just that—give care to their children. Tragically, for many of us, our childhood caregivers also produced significant trauma. Physical, sexual, and emotional abuse are rampant among American families.

The most common effects of these types of abuse—isolation, fear, an inability to trust—can translate into lifelong relational, psychological, and physiological consequences.

Researchers have found that children who experienced abuse and childhood trauma are at higher risk for severe developmental challenges such as cognitive problems, including grade repetition. (Felitti, et al, 1998)

The researchers found that there are substantial physical effects as well. Physically, emotionally, and sexually abused children are reported to have significantly more hospitalizations for illnesses, a greater number of physical and psychological problems, and lower ratings of overall health throughout their lifetime. The greater the number of childhood abuses, the poorer one's adult health and the more likely one will experience abuse as an adult.

Children may develop a variety of disorders to cope with the trauma of their abuse. Some of the most common emotional and behavioral effects include the following:

- Eating disorders
- Drug and alcohol addiction
- Sexual addictions and disorders
- Workaholism
- Self-harm
- Trouble sleeping

- Discomfort with physical touch

- Suppressing traumatizing memories

- Depression, anxiety, other psychiatric disorders

Even children who were not physically hurt but who witnessed domestic violence or abuse in their homes are at an increased risk for emotional and behavioral problems, including anxiety, depression, and academic issues.

> Religious homes can have an equally devastating effect on children. Refer to chapter 11.

According to a 2011 study published by Elsevier, abusive parents often experienced abuse during their own childhoods. Children who experienced physical abuse are significantly more likely to become perpetrators of youth violence than those who did not. Children who have experienced abuse are nine times more likely to become involved in criminal activities. Effects of child sexual abuse can be devastating in adulthood. In addition to the immense guilt, shame, and sense of worthlessness common among those who have been sexually abused, they can also feel powerless and distrustful of others. Sexual abuse often disrupts a person's ability to have normal sexual and emotional relationships. People who have been victims of prolonged sexual abuse commonly struggle with low self-esteem (feeling "dirty") and struggle with abnormal or distorted views of sex. They may show fear and anxiety in response to people who share characteristics of their abuser (the same sex as the abuser, similar physical characteristics, etc.). Those with a prior history of sexual victimization are extremely likely to be re-victimized. Some research estimates an increased risk of over 100 percent. (Hall, 2011)

EMOTIONAL NEGLECT

It's harder to pinpoint, but perhaps even more harmful may be emotional neglect. The effects are prolonged and often underestimated. Children's hearts are born for love and affection like their bodies are born for air. If air is removed, the body suffocates. If love and affection are not available in healthy ways, the soul suffocates.

Emotional neglect may feel puzzling to identify, particularly if it happened in your own life. Emotional neglect is the result of a failure to demonstrate emotion and affection to a child from one who should provide it, such as a parent. If healthy emotion and affection were missing in your life, you were left without a picture of human thriving and connection.

In many ways, long-term emotional neglect is as great a stress as a physical beating. When a child is physically abused, they are at least noticed or acknowledged in some way. When someone is not noticed or acknowledged, they live in a vacuum. They don't exist in a way that gives substance and worth to their being. The human heart was not designed to live in a relational vacuum.

NORMAL CHILDLIKE DEFENSES

Simply being a child is stressful, with the typical stressors of school, relational conflict, physical discomfort, lack of finances, and many other situations. However, when the home is not a place of safety and security, children find themselves on an island of anxiety with no safe place to run for comfort and reassurance. Abnormal long-term stress creates devastating, extended effects.

It is psychologically significant to understand that normal children employ normal defenses when subjected to abnormal long-term stresses. They protect themselves, which is absolutely normal in a high-stress, adverse environment they cannot control.

A child growing up in a stress-filled atmosphere will instinctively look for methods and defenses to lower their stress. The defenses will be quite childlike—preoccupation (video games, internet, television, music, etc.), avoiding being at home, lying, self-blame, rebellion, isolation, and perfectionism. As they enter their teen years, they may become more sophisticated in their defenses and survival techniques, using drugs or alcohol to kill the pain. The child will look for some way to reduce the pain inside them, which is a very normal defense.

When the child becomes an adult and stress hits again, the adult, as if on autopilot, will often instinctively go back to what they did as a child. While growing up, they lacked a healthy model of how to deal with stress on a daily basis. Usually, when we are anxious, nervous, or afraid, we do not instinctively reflect philosophically on what we should do. We simply do what has worked for us during our past life experiences.

NORMAL DEFENSES FOR ADULTS

Imagine if you were a soldier taken prisoner by the enemy and placed in confinement. In confinement you are abused: beaten, attacked, insulted, spit upon. What efforts do you, a soldier, make to protect yourself? The first normal defense you employ is probably to isolate yourself from your abusers whenever you can.

Isolating is a normal response. If your captors ask you a question, you lie, telling them what they want to hear to appear cooperative, lowering the likelihood of threats and harm against you. This would be an understandable and normal defense.

If the guard eyes you and asks, "Do you love our prison?" you respond carefully, "I just love everything about your prison. It is a wonderful, wonderful place."

Anyone watching these scenes would understand, sympathize, appreciate your efforts, and not blame you for these defenses. All these maneuvers can be seen for what they are: forms of self-protection.

For a child in a dysfunctional home, sadly he or she may have parents who often behave like terrorist captors. Unlike a mature soldier, however, the child does not have mature perspectives to draw upon in order to cope, and the child is not suffering for any noble cause. The child is struggling to make sense of the world as they grow, without the gift of knowing that the world in their home is not healthy.

A child uses normal defenses when under threat, just as a soldier uses normal defenses under threat. However, there is another profound difference between being a prisoner in a foreign country and being a prisoner in your home: imprisonment in another country may end, perhaps within a few years. But for a child in a stress-riddled home, it may not end until they're 21 years old. At no time during their growing-up would they have known what normal is. For a child in a dysfunctional home, stress and self-defense are a normal experience; love, joy, and peace are an abnormal experience.

QUESTIONS

Write the top three or four words that would best describe your family members (dad, mom, siblings, step parent, etc.). If you had other primary caregivers (grandparents, etc.) please include them in this reflection question.

_____

_____

_____

_____

Briefly describe the average family scene around the dinner table when you were between the ages of 8 and 10. Capture your response in words, pictures, or symbols.

_____

_____

_____

_____

What are your top three most joyous life events between 4 and 18 years of age? How many of these events were oriented around or involved family?

1. _____

2. _____

3. _____

Describe your top three most difficult life events between 4 and 18 years of age. How many of these events were oriented around or involved family?

1. _____

2. _____

3. _____

CHAPTER 3

The Effects of the Hurting Home

We were designed by God for connection. In fact, psychological and neurological brain research supports the notion that we are hard-wired for relationships. (Lieberman, 2013) We are healthier and happier in every way when we are in connection with others—we are better mentally, emotionally, physically, and spiritually. If this is true, then anything that threatens our ability to connect with others threatens us on a fundamental level.

As children, many of us engaged in life with arms and hearts wide open, reaching out for the love and warmth for which our souls were created.

Then pain came. Unkindness. Disappointment. Perhaps abuse or neglect. Disconnection from those we loved. So we learned to protect ourselves. We did whatever it took, carefully changing our-selves to handle the blows life brought us.

Over time, our protection became armor. Now, we might wear it with certain people in certain moments. Maybe we wear it all day. But, eventually, we can no longer tell the difference between the dented armor and our own skin. And if the armor isn't enough, we build a fortress to keep ourselves safe, or maybe to keep others safe from us. It happened so naturally. Life was hard, but we made it! We lived. We learned to survive, but we didn't learn how to thrive.

NORMAL DOES NOT EQUAL HEALTHY

Our childhoods are the foundation on which our entire lives are built, as Curt Thompson points out in his book *Anatomy of the Soul*. To survive in a home devoid of rich, consistent parental love, healthy limits, and trust-building, children quickly develop survival skills. When children experience a daily environment of unpredictability, chaos, fear, abandonment, denial, and real or potential violence, survival becomes a full-time job.

Survival, by any means, is *normal*.

It is very important to understand, particularly if you suspect you come from a stressed family background, that people commonly beat themselves up for behaviors they learned while growing up. They don't realize these behaviors are simply normal responses to abnormal stresses.

Keep imagining yourself being held captive by an enemy. The things you would do as a captive to survive are the same things a child would do to survive. There are common external and internal responses in these types of painful environments. Please know there is no shame or judgment attached to any of these protection and survival strategies.

The home should not be a place where our survival instincts (fight, flight, or freeze responses) are constantly being triggered.

COMMON EXTERNAL RESPONSES TO STRESS AND PAIN

The results of growing up in a dysfunctional home can be observed both from the child's external responses to stress and pain and from their internal responses to stress and pain. Let's explore these in more detail.

What common external responses does a child in a dysfunctional home develop to survive?

Isolation

A door closing may not provoke an emotional response from you, but for Mike it does. In Mike's childhood home, he could tell what kind of mood his dad was in by how his dad closed the door when he came home from work. If the door closed gently and he was whistling, all was well. But if the door slammed shut and there was the sound of stomping, all the siblings would instinctively scatter.

"Somehow we would all just disappear," Mike said. Mike and his siblings went into seclusion. That door slam was a well-known indicator of his dad's mood. Mike said they would all just leave his mom by herself to deal with dad, which usually did not go well for her. As their mom took the brunt of things, all the kids learned to get as far away from their dad as possible when he was in a bad mood. Like a captive in a foreign country, they would naturally try to isolate themselves from their captor.

It is the normal response for family members to use the method of seclusion to deal with stress. If someone is hurting you, and you are unable to defend yourself against them, you get away from the threat. You figure out a way to become invisible. This is one of the most common external responses a person from a dysfunctional home will develop. It is also one of the most difficult patterns to break once a person becomes an adult.

Avoiding Truth or Lying

Jared struggled with lying. He said, "I tell lies even when I don't have to." After processing it with some good friends, he discovered why. His parents divorced when he was 8 years old. Both his mom and dad remarried. Jared quickly discovered that both sets of parents had high expectations for him. The two sets of expectations were not only very high, but also very different. He found the only way he was going to survive his multiple-family situation was to lie.

He explained, "I would tell them what they wanted to hear so they would leave me alone and I wouldn't get into trouble. Or maybe I adjusted parts of my story to keep them from knowing the whole picture." Truth was not an option. The truth was he could not possibly live up to both sets of parents' expectations. The normal defense any 8-year-old would use is the same defense a captive would use: lie or avoid the whole truth in order to survive. As a form of self-protection, you tell your captors what they want to hear.

Manipulation

In a dysfunctional home, you quickly learn that truth and direct communication are not helpful in getting what you want or need; truth and words are simply weapons you use to survive. In a stress-filled home, there are no ethics; there is only survival. How can you be ethical when you have no ethical resources?

In this type of environment, manipulation is an act of intelligence. Survival means learning the art of manipulating others. You use indirect tactics to manage the emotions, behaviors, and relationships of those around you. This is the mode of operation in the dysfunctional home. You become hyper-vigilant, and begin to learn the weaknesses of those around you in order to take advantage of them and get what you need to survive.

Preoccupation (overworking, accomplishments, sex, pleasure seeking, etc.)

In a dysfunctional home, a child feels tremendous amounts of pain and stress. A very typical way to deal with these feelings is to find something on which you can fixate your mind.

John McCain was a prisoner of war for five and a half years. His first-person account of his ordeal, *John McCain, Prisoner of War*, was published in *U.S. News & World Report* in May, 1973. He said, "It's vital to keep your mind occupied [in order to survive a prisoner-of-war camp] and we all worked on that. Some guys were interested in mathematics, so they worked out complex formulas in their heads—we were never allowed to have writing materials. Others would build a whole house, from basement on up. . . . I spent days on end going back over history books in my mind, figuring out where this country or that country went wrong, what the U. S. should do in the area of foreign affairs . . . It was easy to lapse into fantasies. I used to write books and plays in my mind, but I doubt that any of them would have been above the level of the cheapest dime novel. During one period while I was in solitary, I memorized the names of all 335 of the men who were then prisoners of war in North Vietnam. I can still remember them."

Like a captive prisoner of war, growing up in a pain-filled family environment as a child will cause you to find a way to preoccupy your mind to keep your pain level down. You will find both internal and external things to preoccupy yourself. Many preteens and teenagers preoccupy their minds with video games and texting their friends. The socially acceptable escapes or preoccupations for adults are work and accomplishments.

People may assume drugs, sex, and alcohol are the main ways kids from dysfunctional homes preoccupy themselves. These are common, but getting good grades at school, performing well in athletics, and working hard are also common ways kids preoccupy. Dysfunctional home environments don't just produce alcoholics and drug addicts; they often produce college-educated workaholics who go on to accomplish amazing things. As great as their accomplishments are, however, their souls are in turmoil. Achievements are a powerful way to preoccupy the mind: you not only numb your pain but you've also done something that gives you a sense of achievement and self-respect.

There are socially acceptable ways of preoccupying the mind, and socially unacceptable ways. One that is not always socially acceptable, at least among Christians, is sex. Sex is a way many have chosen to preoccupy their minds from stress and pain and experience pleasure. If you're under a lot of pain and stress, to preoccupy and comfort yourself you might consider the possibility of different types of sexuality you never would have dreamed of outside of being held hostage. You're desperate for anything that distracts your thoughts. Stressful atmospheres often generate sexual aberrations because you have to find something to do in order to get through the pressure you are under.

There's a myriad of things that people have found to preoccupy their minds. But whether they are socially acceptable or unacceptable, make no mistake about it: these behaviors, thoughts, and approaches have been developed to deal unhealthfully with pain and stress. These patterns need to be addressed for a person to be truly healthy emotionally, physically, spiritually, and relationally.

COMMON INTERNAL RESPONSES TO STRESS AND PAIN

While our instinctive external responses definitely affect our lives, our internal responses to stress and pain are even deeper and more life-affecting.

Self-Condemnation

From her early childhood and throughout her teen years, Mary was told she was a problem. She could not remember her parents ever giving her a compliment. Her father regularly worked 60 hours a week. Mary's mom was an accountant for a growing company. Both parents would arrive home late each evening, exhausted. She learned not to ask anything from them because any request was met with short answers, disappointment, and anger.

Mary began to embrace the deep belief that she was not worth her parents' time and affection. She instinctively believed there was something wrong with her that warranted her parents' response to her. During her middle school years, her classmates would tease her and were mean to her, further supporting the belief that something was wrong with her. She regularly called herself derogatory names.

Mary became sexually active in her early teens. Gaining this form of attention from teen boys was at least some kind of affection and value that she desperately needed. She also found acceptance from peers and relief from her self-disdain through drug use. However, her behavior led to more guilt, shame, and self-condemnation. Her mother found a stash of drugs in Mary's room, leading to further condemnation and rejection from her parents.

As an adult, Mary recounted, "The strange thing is, I instinctively thought I deserved the rejection I was experiencing. Rejection lined up with what I believed about myself."

Dysfunctional homes are factories for self-blame and condemnation. They are the natural by-product of an unloving, unaffectionate home. Our hearts and minds have to make some sense out of our experiences. Our fallen instincts want to attach blame onto something or someone. For most of us, the logical conclusion that ties everything together is that we are the common denominator. We think, "There must be something wrong with me."

Similarly, an adult woman who is raped will spend a year or two trying to make sense of herself and the experience. Sadly, most of the time, she'll struggle with self-blame even though it was done to her by an abuser who acted out of his own fallen instincts. Self-blame is a natural, internal response to a stress-filled home environment.

Living in Shame

Another natural internal response to a dysfunctional family is shame. Shame is different from guilt. Guilt is an internal pain as a result of something you have done. Shame is pain over who you are, as opposed to what you do.

As an abused child, you don't understand exactly why things are so screwed up in the family, so you conclude the problem must be you. It was because of who you are as a person. You wind up ashamed of who you are, because you must be pretty low and cruddy to merit the treatment you are receiving. When people conclude they need to hide who they are, they go into deep shame. Shame drives them to isolate further.

Hiding hurts us; people who go in hiding are not truly known by anyone. Because they are not letting others know them and their hurt, they can't be helped. They can't be loved when they are alone. They don't even know themselves deeply. They become stranded on a deserted island of pain and they don't like the company they are stuck with—themselves. When you come from a dysfunctional home, shame is one of the greatest inner-life obstacles to overcome to receive help.

Shutting Down Emotion

When you live in a stressful home you may quickly learn an alternative to constant emotional pain and trauma: simply stop feeling. As a child, you are not sophisticated enough to sort through your emotions, especially when you live in constant relational stress and pain. To cope, most of us simply stop feeling.

The problem with this approach is that it is difficult, if not impossible, to select which emotions you no longer want to feel. In our attempt to suppress our emotions in general, both painful and pleasurable emotions are suppressed. We learn to not feel the painful emotions yet wonder what happened to our joy.

When we enter adulthood practicing this skill year after year, we find ourselves struggling to feel *anything*. Like the character of Spock on *Star Trek*, our approach to life becomes pure thought, reason, and behavior. We think it works for us, so what's the big deal? It becomes an issue when we enter into relationships with others. To the people in our lives, we may seem distant, cold, and impersonal. Emotions—the very thing we have been suppressing—are what animate us, making us warm and approachable. Suppressing our emotions makes us cold and mechanical, even appearing to be judgmental.

Lack of Trust for Others

When you are in a pain-filled, chaotic home, you learn that trust is not a good choice. When your parents or other family members have betrayed you, you learn not to expect the best out of people. A person from a dysfunctional home learns that trusting people sets you up for more disappointment and pain. When people from this type of background get married, they have the tendency to bring all that suspicion into their marriage, as well as into their other adult relationships.

Assuming Communication Is Useless

In a dysfunctional home, communication solves nothing. In a hurting home, truth-telling doesn't build trust: it brings us more pain. Numerous interactions with family members where communication regularly generates pain show us that communication solves nothing.

A teen dares not let their parents know he or she is struggling in school because they learned it would quickly be met with yelling and disciplinary action instead of compassion and understanding. In a dysfunctional home, communication becomes the doorway to more pain. Avoidance appears to be the doorway to peace.

Unfortunately, it may not be until much later in life that we learn that communication avoidance is also the doorway to loneliness and isolation. This belief and instinct that communication solves nothing doesn't just disappear during adulthood. We must become more aware of our tendency toward non-communication and sort out our instincts concerning this vital relational skill.

Creating a False Self

A common internal response to pain and stress is the creation of a false self. False self is when a person embraces false views, perceptions, and ideas about who they are and what they are worth.

A common example of this is what happens in the mind of a child when they watch their parents fight. Instinctively, children typically believe the reason their parents fight is because of them.

Children will think, "If I was a better child, my parents wouldn't fight." The false self is the child's belief that they are the problem.

As a child, you begin to develop the mentality of blaming yourself for what is happening in the home. Children who learn to blame themselves develop the characteristics of a victim mentality. As a result, they create a person within themselves to explain what's going on outside; they create someone who's worthy of the type of treatment they are receiving.

The creation of a false self is a natural result of this type of environment. It's amazing how many of us go into adulthood carrying the belief that in any given situation we are the problem. For most of us this sense of false self was developed when we were very young.

As early as Annie could remember, she was continually told by her mother that she was overweight. Every time Annie looked in the mirror all she could see was a "fat" 6-year-old. As a teen, who was actually more thin than overweight, going into her 20s, she had the instinctive belief that she was fat. This false self eventually led to a struggle with bulimia. Her false self kept Annie from enjoying beach outings and taking pictures with friends and family. Intimacy with her husband became a struggle.

Annie said, "When I feel 'fat' or 'ugly' the last thing I want is for my husband to see me or be with me. I don't feel lovable or worthy of his attention."

Unhealthy religious home environments also powerfully create false views of self: Imagine a home where it becomes very apparent that bad decisions and mistakes quickly make you an unacceptable person. Unhealthy religious homes are heavy with behavioral expectations. As a child, you either rebel against this atmosphere or quickly figure out a way to appear to be a person who pleases the authority figure in the home.

Mom and Dad typically model the use of false self: they may fight like cats and dogs before church, but when they walk through the church doors, they suddenly paste smiles on their faces, looking and sounding like peaceful, joyful Christians. Once out of church and back in the car, they're back to their normal, stressed-out selves. Children pick up on this behavior quickly. They learn what is acceptable and not acceptable, and the creation of a false self is modeled by their parents as the answer.

We call this condition the "false self," but the Bible uses the word *hypocrisy*. The word *hypocrite* comes from a Greek word meaning an actor who wears a mask in theatrical plays. Just like the ancient Greek actor, we practice being someone else; when it's time to survive, the mask goes on, and the act begins.

THE RELATIONAL RESULTS OF DYSFUNCTIONAL FAMILY BACKGROUNDS

Poor Skills Expressing Emotions

Those who grow up in a dysfunctional home often have poor skills expressing love or even saying a heartfelt statement like "I love you," to someone close. In a hurting home, it's typical to rarely hear those words expressed in a healthy way. As a result, many of us from dysfunctional homes have very poor skills expressing positive emotions to others.

During my childhood, my dad rarely, if ever, told me he loved me. If you knew my father's background you would quickly understand why that was a difficult thing for him to do. As a result, I did not have the experience of my dad embracing me as his son, looking me deep in the eyes and telling me that he loved me.

I became a Christian during my freshman year in college. As a new Christian, I was invited to spend time with families who attended my church. Right after my wife, Renee, and I were married, one family in particular, Dave and Kris Schmidt, often invited us into their home. Dave was a man's man. He hunted, fished, and drove a big four-wheel drive pickup. But I consistently observed Dave doing something that disturbed me. Dave and Kris had three children, two boys and one girl. At that time, all three kids were under the age of 10. Dave would often scoop up his little boys, lift them up in the air, and start kissing them all over their face and hugging them, swinging them around and smiling at them, saying he loved them so much. I remember once as he was doing that, he turned to me with a big smile and said, "Tim, you can't love them enough. They need so much love."

I remember leaving that night with Renee and telling her, "I think I need to confront Dave about what he is doing to his boys. He doesn't realize that he is likely going to make them gay." I know that sounds silly, but that is what I instinctually thought he was doing. A father hugging and kissing his sons on the face was so far from my home experience. It really wasn't until I had my own sons that I realized I was the one who was missing something that I should have gotten. I quickly realized that I didn't know how to receive or relate to positive emotions. I had poor skills at expressing emotions to my sons.

People who come from dysfunctional homes may not only have poor skills expressing positive emotions, but also poor skills expressing negative emotions. The way negative emotions were expressed in my family background was by yelling, blaming, hitting, cursing, or simply avoiding communication all together. Healthy ways of expressing negative feelings were not modeled in the home where I grew up. Talking about what I was feeling was an extremely novel thought.

Poor Skills Expressing Affection

A person who has not been shown healthy physical affection while growing up will likely struggle relationally. Consider how environments lacking healthy affection can deeply, negatively impact a person.

Imagine a home where a child was shown no affection, where the affection shown was manipulative, where affection came in the form of sexual abuse, where affection was shown only when they performed well, or where they received affection only when their parent was drunk. Scenarios like these impact a person's view of physical affection and its role in relationships. A background like this certainly inhibits one's ability to express healthy affection to their spouse, children, and other significant relationships.

Poor Problem-Solving Skills

Growing up, I didn't know how to work through relational problems. Daily relationships require a lot of communication. What was modeled to me was posturing, strong-arming, yelling, manipulation, and/or avoidance when there was a problem. The idea of talking through a relational issue was absolutely not part of my home environment.

Problem solving involves listening and caring about what another person thinks. Listening and caring for another's thoughts and feelings were not modeled to us in my childhood home. Frequently, people who grow up in dysfunctional homes feel at home with chaos. When things get crazy, people from dysfunctional families actually begin to feel more at home, even peaceful. Why? Because chaos feels like home. They know how to handle chaos. But this is not the same as being well-equipped with problem-solving skills.

While in ministry with Campus Crusade, I worked closely with a leader who seemed to create chaos wherever he went. It drove me and the others who worked closely with him crazy. I later learned why he did this. He felt at home in chaos. He was more comfortable in that type of work environment, versus the controlled, even-tempered work environment the rest of us desired. He shined during relational chaos. However, during conflicts where there was heartfelt, calm communication, he fell apart and felt very uncomfortable.

MARKS OF AN UNHEALTHY FAMILY EXPLAINED

In summary, here are some of the most common characteristics of a dysfunctional home:

Unloving: A primary characteristic that marks an unhealthy family environment is a general sense among family members that the environment lacks the feeling of love. This is a general category into which all the unhealthy characteristics on these pages fall. Family members in an unloving family environment feel they are not delighted in or cared for. The biblical qualities of love talked about in 1 Corinthians 13:1-13 (patience, kindness, others-centered, long-suffering, positive and believing spirit, hope, etc.) are lacking or not present at all.

Compulsive: Compulsive behavior is a rut where people, instead of living freely, allow inner tensions, urges, moods, and desires to control them and their family relationships. From a biblical perspective, we call this living according to the desires of the flesh and the mind (Ephesians 2:1-3). Compulsive behavior is when satisfying a mood or strong desire is more important than the well-being of self or others. Compulsive behavior is apparent. For example, the mom who continually nags her children and/or husband without reflecting on or considering the relational issues has determined that expressing her mood is more important than the impact of her words on the family.

Critical: A family member who is critical communicates to other family members that they are unacceptable as a person. It's often without rhyme or reason. Their criticism of others is likely a result of the turmoil they feel within or about themselves. Chances are they were wounded as a child, and they carry that wound in their subconscious. Though not aware of the wound, it makes them overly-critical and unbearable to be around. Negative messages they may have constantly received as a child turned into a way of thinking that leads them to be an overly-critical and sarcastic adult. In reality, criticism of others is an effort to somehow make themselves feel better (often on a subconscious level). Unfortunately, the result of their critical spirit drives others from them, causing more inner pain and turmoil, which they continue to mismanage through their criticism of others.

Indirect Communication (lying): This is when people within the family do not say things that reflect reality. They develop a pattern of ignoring the truth to avoid pain. In an unhealthy family, it is not acceptable to say what a family member really feels or thinks. It is innately known among family that reality is not to be spoken of—living in denial is more comfortable. There is a strong sense of shame that drives this behavior. Family members who feel shame want to hide the part of themselves that feels unacceptable.

Inflexible: A family member that is inflexible tends to be a dominating personality who must get his or her desires met in order to keep the peace. Change is difficult for this family member. There is a tendency for this person to believe if something changes within their system of coping mechanisms, then the balance of the universe will somehow be thrown into chaos and disaster may come upon them and others. The tendency of being inflexible can also be the basis for the characteristic of being controlling.

Controlling: A tremendous level of control goes on in an unhealthy family. Strong-arming and manipulation are commonplace. Fear and anger are the dominant emotions leading to control or manipulation of other family members. Usually a controlling family member has a conscious and unconscious list of fears or anxieties to which they and others are responding.

Ungrateful: There is a sense of want, discontentment, and dissatisfaction among members of an unhealthy family. The glass is half empty, not half full. People look more at their circumstances rather than other family members and their well-being. If a person is dealing with long-term stress and relational and emotional pain, it creates an atmosphere of survival, not gratefulness.

Non-Affectionate: Regular, ongoing expression of healthy affection is noticeably missing in unhealthy families. Displays of affection may be sparsely present but are normally attributed to an act of manipulation, are mood-based, or are in correlation with a family member being under the influence of alcohol or drugs. Withholding affection is also a tool used among unhealthy families to either punish or manipulate other family members.

Distrustful: In unhealthy families, trust simply means a lower level of suspicion. When there is a pattern of family members hurting each other, empty promises are given on a regular basis, and compulsive behavior seems to be what determines actions. Trust becomes an unwise choice among members of the unhealthy family.

Self-Centered: There is an inability to focus on others in unhealthy families. Personal pain naturally draws the family members to focus on themselves. It is difficult to see another person's need through the eyes of someone who hurts, is without comfort, and who lacks a healthy perspective about their pain.

Performance-Oriented: Performance-oriented family members communicate that what you do is far more significant than who you are. If you get the right grades, do your piano lessons, or have the right friends, you are acceptable. It is like a family member who carries a scorecard in their back pocket, so to speak. If you score high enough, there is a sense of acceptance; if the score is low, then it is directly or indirectly (nonverbally) communicated that you are not acceptable. Performance-oriented families often produce family members who go into hiding (lying or running away) and/or performers. It is natural for someone who cannot live up to the expectations of their family to create a false self or false reality in order to gain the family's acceptance.

Unforgiving: This family environment does not let go of the hurt done to them. Family members continue to relive moments that hurt them. In doing so, they recharge their original emotions about the event. A deep sense of justice and/or injustice fuels this home. Blaming is an unhealthy communication pattern often used by family members in an unforgiving home environment. Their well-rehearsed belief is that their hurt and inner turmoil are a result of those around them and those they mistakenly trusted in their past.

Inconsistent: An important ingredient in raising healthy children is a consistent home environment where parents' love, affection, expectations, discipline, etc. are predictable. When they are unpredictable, the child becomes heavily stressed and goes into crisis. The dysfunctional home environment is chaotic. Family members are inconsistent in response to relational and emotional pain. Expressions of love, affection, expectations, and discipline come out of their chaotic inner life, which overflows into their parenting, creating an inconsistent home environment.

Lacking Positive Emotions: When the home environment is constantly painful and emotions are shut down or mismanaged, it has a profoundly negative impact on a child. Lack of consistent positive emotions can be extremely painful and damaging. Often when a child experiences prolonged emotional pain they must find a way to somehow cope and function in spite of what they are feeling. A child will typically deal with their painful emotions by shutting down, performing, medicating/satiating, preoccupying, or resorting to other unhealthy behaviors.

QUESTIONS

Is it easy or difficult for you to revisit memories of your childhood or family background? If it is difficult, why do you think that is?

_____

_____

_____

_____

_____

What were some of the common *external* defenses you used to protect yourself during your childhood? Do you relate to any of these external responses to stress and pain? (Examples: lying, isolation, manipulation, preoccupation, hitting, yelling, ignoring, etc.)

_____

_____

_____

_____

_____

What were some of the common *internal* defenses you used to protect yourself during your childhood? Do you relate to any of these internal responses to stress and pain? (Examples: self-condemnation, shame, shutting down of emotions, false self, assuming communication is useless, etc.)

_____

_____

_____

_____

_____

Do you see any of these external or internal responses to stress show-ing up in your tendencies toward your current relationships? If so, what are they specifically?

_____

_____

_____

_____

_____

CHAPTER 4

Dysfunctional Backgrounds and the Bible

Make no mistake about it—God has great compassion for the dysfunctional home. The Bible expresses God's heart and deep concern for hurting families. The scriptures talk about dysfunctional homes, however it does not refer to them in our modern day vernacular. So we must look more closely to unlock its insights.

In the New Testament, the apostle Paul describes the problems of human life. In Romans 3, he observes human beings and their instinctive relationship to God the Father:

> "There is none righteous, not even one; there is none who understands, there is none who seeks for God; all have turned aside, together they have become useless; there is none who does good, there is not even one."
>
> —Romans 3:10-12 (NASB 1995)

The nature of mankind and the history of the fall in the garden make clear that "together they have become useless." The Greek word used for useless is ἀχρειόω. It means "rendered useless." This verb is derived from the Greek noun for "hand." The thought is that the hand was not functioning as it should, and therefore useless. In other words, everyone has stopped functioning correctly. It would be a completely legitimate translation to say, "Together they have all become dysfunctional." "They" includes all of humanity and all its families, groups, and human relationships. The word useless means "it does not work."

Something useless is not functioning as it ought. Anything that is broken to the point that it no longer works as designed is useless. It's functionality becomes twisted or lost. The Bible recognizes, as does modern clinical research, that mankind has a terrible problem. Families, cultures, and people are not functioning correctly. Dysfunction is normative more times than not, and the effects are devastating.

Not acknowledging our dysfunction and brokenness will simply deepen our pain and frustration. Most of us have experiences with people and situations in our lives that clearly are not working as they ought. Amazingly, though, we usually continue pretending all is well. My daughter, Aubrey, had injured her arm several times as a child. After breaking her wrist yet again one day, she did not want to go to the doctor; she tried to hide her arm's uselessness from her mother and me. When we pressed her to admit something was wrong and asked her to pick up a cup off the table, she tried to prove her wrist was fine by scooting the cup around with the back of her hand. Try as she might to hide it, it was obvious her hand wasn't functioning properly. She provided a living example of what Romans 3:10-12 was referring to with the word "useless."

THE BIBLE ACKNOWLEDGES THE IMPACT OF A FALL-EN FAMILY BACKGROUND

The answers in the Bible communicate unequivocally that your background can prepare you for emotional and relational success or failure in your adult life. Proverbs 30 speaks about how a person's background affects their current relationships.

> Under three things the earth trembles; under four it cannot bear up: a slave when he becomes king, and a fool when he is filled with food; an unloved woman when she gets a husband, and a maidservant when she displaces her mistress.

—Proverbs 30:21-23 (ESV)

In Proverbs 30, three events cause earthquakes; a fourth event is such a catastrophe, the earth cannot even stand and the ground gives way.

Verse 22 is our first earthquake: "a slave when he becomes king." A man with the social background of slavery, ordered about and beaten, is not an individual who should be given authority. A slave during Old and New Testament times developed a slave-type mentality. Why not place such a person in great authority? Well, what would be the desire of a slave? A position of power, where the cruel wrongs of their life could be avenged. They may say to themselves, "If I become king, I will do what I want, and I will right all wrongs done to me. Heads will roll, and I will finally get the respect that I deserve."

Another earthquake occurs as we see "a fool when he is filled with food." This is the Bible's picture of codependency. When people who have a long-term pattern of making foolish decisions are supported and provided for in a way that allows those foolish, poor choices to continue, the ground around them becomes unstable. What happens in the dynamic of parents supplying funds for a son living with a tragic drug addiction, or of the wife of a 900-pound man continuing to provide the unhealthy food he requests?

All the people involved know better, but blind spots and unhealthy interactions keep the "fool" isolated from the consequences of their actions. They remain isolated until the effects can no longer be contained, resulting in an ensuing tragedy. The earth trembles when a fool is empowered in their bad decision-making.

A third earthquake is seen as the author illustrates the effects of an individual raised in a dysfunctional family environment becoming an adult and marrying. Though a modern Bible translation reads, "the earth trembles under . . . an unloved woman when she gets a husband," it could legitimately be translated: "A massive earthquake will inevitably hit under a continually hated or abused woman when she gets a husband." The image captures the painful calamity of a young woman who grows up in an abusive home and does not receive the love and care one should experience in the home environment. A woman (or man) who is continually neglected or abused will struggle not only to sort out the pain planted by her family, but will lack the perspective and skills for a healthy marriage and future relationships.

One of the most enduring injuries of a dysfunctional family background is how it affects our ability to connect with others. The tragedy we experienced in childhood was pain, but the current and coming earthquake in adulthood due to a lack of healthy relational skills and perspectives results in more relational grief. At first glance, the woman (or man) as talked about in Proverbs 30 may appear functional, but in an intimate relationship, she (or he) is without the ability to make real connection. Chances are the following are true:

- She does not know what love is (how to give or receive it).

- She lacks a positive identity and sense of self-worth.

- She does not know the benefits of trust.

- She does not know the benefits of forgiveness.

- She lacks basic communication skills.

- She lacks basic conflict resolution skills.

- She cannot comfort herself in healthy ways.

It's likely her greatest desire was to escape her painful home and find the white knight who would care for her. Unfortunately, there is a problem, and the problem has been created within her. Our experiences and family health statistics tell us there are people reading this who are still shaking from experiencing this earthquake firsthand.

WHEN THE EARTH GIVES WAY

The author of Proverbs 30 draws a final terrible picture: the earth crumbles and completely falls away when a maidservant displaces her mistress. The maidservant swims in the pain of all three worlds: the slave, the fool, and the unloved woman.

A maidservant has not been treated warmly; she was expected to serve at the command and whim of another and has not had the experience of receiving consideration or care. She was a tool in the service of the house and its owners. She was always less than a full person in her own right. She may even have been abused. When she displaces her mistress, the head of the household, she now holds sway over a husband, a family, and a household of servants. The desire to exert never-before-held power will be tremendous. She is like a slave becoming a king, going from abuse to now being in a

position of authority. It is likely she will rule the house and its oc-
cupants unwisely, perhaps even cruelly.

She also suffers the pain of the fool who is inappropriately satisfied with whatever the passing whims of her heart may be. Rather
than knowing how to seek lasting joy and intimacy, quickly received
and quickly passing satisfactions like food and money will seem like
the answers to her heart, particularly because she may not have enjoyed these luxuries previously. She might even use these things to
try to sway others to follow her.

Now, she has not only been thrust into a position of power but
also the position of a wife as she has taken the place of the wife and
mother of the household. The wife is the role of a woman meant to
be loved. A wife only thrives when she trusts that she is loved and
that love motivates all her husband does for her. For a maidservant,
selfless love is probably something with which she has no experience. She has no paradigm for trust. Love has not been the motivation for anything she has experienced before; survival has been her
motivation and she used her obedience to stay alive. She doesn't
have relational skills; she only has obedience skills. Her ability to
enjoy, to trust, to receive well—which is the foundation for giving
well to others—is crippled.

She is a used woman, an unloved woman, who still has a deep
longing for real intimacy. But nothing in her training or background
has prepared her with the skills she needs to accept intimacy, to
relate well to others, or to use the material things of life in appropriate ways. She is utterly isolated and constantly in a mode of self-
protection, of both her position and her heart.

Though a woman is mentioned in the verse, the principle holds equally true for a man. A continually mistreated son can result in a tough, bulletproof man, the making of a driven athlete or soldier. However, he will likely lack the inner life and relational skills to be a loving husband and father. There is simply a whole range of skills and relational abilities missing. Sooner or later, as a result, earthquakes occur that shock and shatter relationships.

Modern psychology observes what God has been saying all along. What happened to us in childhood and in our families of origin matters. Because of our fallen backgrounds, we live with deficiencies that affect our current relationships.

- The slave does not have the life experience to bring wisdom to a kingdom.

- The fool does not learn natural consequences of choices and pursuits.

- The unloved woman (or man) never experienced giving or receiving trusted love.

- The maidservant, similar to the slave king, the fool, and unloved woman, is crippled by her background, struggling to love well and relate in a healthy way.

GOD TAKES SERIOUSLY WHAT HAPPENS IN THE HOME. HE UNDERSTANDS CHILDHOOD PAIN!

An important question we need to address is "Where is God in all of this?" Where is God when children are experiencing horror in these types of home environments? What is his perspective toward the situations in our culture and homes?

Those from hurting homes may have resentments toward God, blaming him for either his lack of care in their situations or for his absence. They may even consider God the culprit for causing the pain because he had the power to stop it but chose not to do so.

It is extremely important to see God's true heart for the hurting home. In brief, God is not a passive Father. His Son, Jesus, is not a distant, uncompassionate observer. If you are from a pain-filled family background, know God deeply cares about what you experienced as a child. He takes seriously what happens in a hurting home. You may ask, "Where was God when I was in such pain during my childhood?" The answer is he was dying on a cross as a ransom for you. The answer is he is a good Father and gave a son for you as payment to adopt you into his family. God said he is not only going to redeem you, the victim, but he is going to redeem both the victim and the victimizer! God's answer to the dysfunctional home is to redeem the whole mess.

Let's look at a passage where Jesus talks about both the child who is the victim and the adult who is the victimizer. In the following passage, Jesus is telling his disciples of his death. One of them asks who will be greatest among them after Jesus is gone. Jesus has a surprising reply about who's greatest in the eyes of God. Read carefully what he says. Notice that Jesus Christ was aware of man's condition. See God's heart for children and how he cares about what happens to them in and outside the home.

> "Truly I say to you, unless you are converted and become like children, you will not enter the kingdom of heaven. Whoever then humbles himself as this child, he is the greatest in the kingdom of heaven. And whoever re-

ceives one such child in My name receives Me; but whoever causes one of these little ones who believe in Me to stumble, it would be better for him to have a heavy millstone hung around his neck, and to be drowned in the depth of the sea."

—Matthew 18:3-6 (NASB 1995)

What does "become like children" mean? An entire book could be written on this subject. Some possible responses could be a healthy dependence, trust, honesty, teachability, and humility with God.

Does God care about what happens to a child? There is perhaps no stronger way to say it. Jesus said in this passage that the way you treat a child is equal to the way you treat him. *He* feels the pain and rejection each mistreated child feels. In my opinion, Jesus could not state it more clearly. He said, "When children are hurt, I hurt. When they are welcomed, I feel as though I am being welcomed." The implications of this are profound.

If you were from a dysfunctional home, he felt your hurt and pain. As a father, I understand this principle. When my children hurt, I hurt. I would much rather have my face be stitched up then watch my 10-year-old son, Spencer, go through that agony in the emergency room. I would much rather be laying in a hospital bed with my arm shattered than watch my 3-year-old daughter, Aubrey, lay in that bed in pain. I would rather have my arm chopped off than watch my adult daughter, Savannah, go through the pain of her divorce. I know this because I've experienced all of these things firsthand.

Note when the Bible makes references to people stumbling, it means people being injured or tripped up by misinformation (verbal and/or nonverbal) that tethers their heart and mind to a lie or false belief.

The term used for the word "stumble" in the original language is *skandalizo*—it's the word from which we get the English word "scandal." (Strong, 1984) Obviously, the word stumble means to trip and fall. The use of "stumble" in the Bible often implies a person is somehow injured or killed.

What is Jesus saying? A very accurate restatement is, "But whoever causes one of these little ones who believe in me to be set up in such a way that as they proceed through life and trip over that which they do not see or understand, and they are injured because of their relationships, is going to suffer in a serious way."

"Stumbling" is used throughout the New Testament. It almost always refers to someone being given misinformation and tethering their heart and mind to a lie that sets them up for a spiritual, emotional, and/or relational disaster.

Jesus communicated how strongly he feels about "stumbled" children when he said it would be better for the victimizer to have a heavy millstone hung around his neck and to be drowned in the depth of the sea. When I spoke on this passage at a conference, a woman came to me in tears afterwards and said, "I know exactly what Jesus meant when he said that statement. I know I've stumbled my children and I can say confidently I would rather have a millstone tied to my neck and be tossed into the sea than stumble my children."

WE REDEFINE WORDS WHEN WE STUMBLE

A person in pain due to a dysfunctional background will begin to redefine words. Words that typically have very positive feelings for those from a healthy family background, such as love, peace, joy, compassion, and trust, take on new meanings for people raised in pain and stress.

Our wounded, stumbled meanings of words and phrases might look like this:

Love:
- Love is what someone says to manipulate us.
- Love is something that will get you hurt.

Trust:
- A person is occasionally reliable.
- Trust is simply a lower level of suspicion.
- Trust is something that will get you killed.

Peace:
- Peace is something we get only when we preoccupy ourselves, or medicate or satiate so we don't think about our past or current pain.
- Peace is something we experience as we perfect shutting down our emotions.

Joy:
- Joy is a momentary feeling when we are able to step out of life's realities.
- Joy is something we felt more as children, when we were young and naïve.

Hope:
- Hope is delayed disappointment.

Compassion:
- Compassion is pity; expected or forced generosity.
- Compassion comes with shame and guilt-driven care.

Trials and Pain:

- Trials and pain are things given *only* to the undeserving, the unloved, and/or the worthless.
- Trials and pain are used only to scorn, punish, and abuse.

"Stumbled" children unfortunately become stumbled adults. What about the stumbling adult?

Jesus follows this vivid picture of his value for children and the costs of stumbling with these words:

> "Woe to the world because of its stumbling blocks! For it is inevitable that stumbling blocks come, but woe to that man through whom the stumbling block comes! If your hand or foot causes you to stumble, cut it off and throw it from you; it is better for you to enter life crippled or lame, than to have two hands or two feet to be cast into the eternal fire. If your eye causes you to stumble, pluck it out and throw it from you. It is better for you to enter life with one eye, than to have two eyes and be cast into the fiery hell. See that you do not despise one of these little ones, for I say to you that their angels in heaven continually see the face of my Father who is in heaven."

> —Matthew 18:7-10 (NASB 1995)

These are difficult words, but Christ's intent is clear: after talking about the seriousness of children who stumble, he talks about stumbling adults and their path toward darkness. Jesus said unless there is radical change, you're on the path toward more darkness. If you continue to walk in the manner in which your stumbling blocks have tripped you, you will continue to be scandalized and walk further into a fallen world.

EVERY VICTIM BECOMES A VICTIMIZER!

The Bible's approach to human behavior is this: every victim becomes a victimizer. People who have been hurt go on to hurt others. This does not mean that if you were sexually abused as a child you will sexually abuse someone else. It does mean that unless your experience of abuse is effectively addressed, sooner or later someone will experience pain in some form (neglect, isolation, physical coldness, etc.) from you.

The horrible thing about the human condition is that if you were deeply hurt as a child (or as an adult) and you do not somehow, in a healthy way, resolve your deep hurt and pain, others around you will eventually experience your hurt in one way or another.

Jesus communicates the seriousness of the condition of adults who were hurt during childhood and how the stumbling cycle should be addressed:

> "And if your hand or your foot is causing you to sin, cut it off and throw it away from you; it is better for you to enter life maimed or without a foot, than to have two hands or two feet and be thrown into the eternal fire. And if your eye is causing you to sin, tear it out and throw it away from you. It is better for you to enter life with one eye, than to have two eyes and be thrown into the fiery hell."

> —Matthew 18:8-9 (NASB 1995)

Note that not one of Jesus' disciples cut off their hands or feet or plucked out their eyes. They didn't do these things literally because they all knew what he was saying. In the Old and New Testaments the hands, feet, and eyes were used in hyperbole: Hands represented what you do. Feet represented where you go, your daily paths, and habits. Eyes represented your perspectives on life.

In Genesis 3, when Eve and Adam ate the fruit God had commanded they not eat, their eyes were opened, and they knew good and evil. It wasn't that their physical eyes were previously closed; it's that their perspective changed. The eye represents perspective, the hand represents what you do, and the feet represent habits of life.

Jesus says if you're an adult and you were "stumbled" as a child, you need to do something as radical as a person who slices off his hand to stop doing what they are doing. He said you need to be as serious about changing your daily habits as the person who would cut off his foot. Stop and change your daily habits. Be as serious about changing your perspective as the person who would pluck out his eye. Change your perspectives about yourself, others, and God. In order to break the stumbling cycle, you are in need of serious, radical change.

OH, NO! I'VE BECOME MY PARENT!

Often as adults it begins to dawn on us that we have become our parents. It is not always a pleasant realization. Befuddled, we ask the question, "How did this happen?"

Firstly, life skills, perspectives, and inner-life dynamics are not taught—they are caught. We learn our life and coping skills from thousands upon thousands of interactions with dysfunctional people.

Secondly, the inner life that resulted from that dysfunctional parent is still very much in chaos and pain. Again, victims become victimizers.

We Need to Know What We Carry So We Can Change

We've covered a poetic description of the dysfunctional lifestyle affecting the child who stumbles, the judgment on the person who causes the stumbling, and the serious situation of the adult who's stumbled. In chapter 6, we'll look at our own particular family background to understand more clearly what we may be carrying into our adult lives as a result. We'll also look at what it takes to bring change.

A Mature Perspective Is Needed

The apostle Paul says in I Corinthians:

> When I was a child, I used to speak like a child, think like a child, reason like a child; when I became a man, I did away with childish things.
>
> —1 Corinthians 13:11 (NASB 1995)

Paul states what seems obvious: when we become adults, we should speak, think, and reason as adults. We should have the perspectives of an adult. However, many of us from hurting homes have not realized how we have been trapped in our pasts. We have not matured in our emotional or relational lives because healthy, effective adult skills were not imparted to us.

From a Christian point of view, we have not brought God's mature perspectives into our childhood experiences so we can be free to move into maturity as believers. Please understand there is no shame or blame in this! A level of inner life and relational deficiencies are realities for most of us. However, I assure you there is hope and healing to come!

QUESTIONS

Have you encountered a person who is an "earthquake" waiting to happen, as is talked about in Proverbs 30:21-23? If so, describe this person.

_____

_____

_____

_____

What do you think of this statement: "Not acknowledging our dysfunction and brokenness will simply deepen our pain and frustration"? Do you think it's true?

_____

_____

_____

_____

Is it easy or difficult for you to acknowledge your own brokenness? Do you believe that you were "stumbled" as a child?

_____

_____

_____

_____

If someone asked you, "Where was God when I was in such pain during my childhood?" according to this chapter, how would you answer them?

_____

_____

_____

_____

CHAPTER 5

A Healthy Home
According to the Bible

This chapter on what a healthy home looks like is brief by design, because many of the attributes of the healthy family will be talked about more starting in chapter 9. But before we can visit our own family backgrounds, we must first understand a few of the broad strokes of what a healthy, functional family looks like. As a Christian, the standard for a healthy home environment is talked about and exemplified to us by God's family (the Trinitarian family of the Father, Son, and Holy Spirit) as described in the Bible. God's family relational environment is the only truly healthy, functional family.

Below, I've listed the major characteristics of God's family as described in the Bible. Again, please note that each one of these family characteristics will be talked about in more detail in the coming chapters. For now, I'll simply list each family characteristic and support it with scripture, allowing God to speak through the Bible passage concerning his family's relational environment.

HEALTHY FAMILY RELATIONAL ENVIRONMENT CHARACTERISTICS

Loving

> Beloved, let us love one another, for love is from God, and
> whoever loves has been born of God and knows God.

Anyone who does not love does not know God, because God is love. In this the love of God was made manifest among us, that God sent his only Son into the world, so that we might live through him. In this is love, not that we have loved God but that he loved us and sent his Son to be the propitiation for our sins.

—1 John 4:7-10 (ESV)

If I speak in the tongues of men and of angels, but have not love, I am a noisy gong or a clanging cymbal. And if I have prophetic powers, and understand all mysteries and all knowledge, and if I have all faith, so as to remove mountains, but have not love, I am nothing. If I give away all I have, and if I deliver up my body to be burned, but have not love, I gain nothing. Love is patient and kind; love does not envy or boast; it is not arrogant or rude. It does not insist on its own way; it is not irritable or resentful; it does not rejoice at wrongdoing, but rejoices with the truth. Love bears all things, believes all things, hopes all things, endures all things. Love never ends. As for prophecies, they will pass away; as for tongues, they will cease; as for knowledge, it will pass away. For we know in part and we prophesy in part, but when the perfect comes, the partial will pass away. When I was a child, I spoke like a child, I thought like a child, I reasoned like a child. When I became a man, I gave up childish ways. For now we see in a mirror dimly, but then face to face. Now I know in part; then I shall know fully, even as I have been fully known. So now faith, hope, and love abide, these three; but the greatest of these is love.

—1 Corinthians 13:1-13 (ESV)

Trusting (Faith)

Now faith (trust) is the assurance of things hoped for, the conviction of things not seen.

—Hebrews 11:1 (ESV)

And without faith (trust) it is impossible to please him, for whoever would draw near to God must believe that he exists and that he rewards those who seek him.

—Hebrews 11:6 (ESV)

For by grace you have been saved through faith (trust). And this is not your own doing; it is the gift of God, not a result of works, so that no one may boast.

—Ephesians 2:8-9 (ESV)

Others-Centered

Do nothing from selfish ambition or conceit, but in humility count others more significant than yourselves. Let each of you look not only to his own interests, but also to the interests of others. Have this mind among yourselves, which is yours in Christ Jesus, who, though he was in the form of God, did not count equality with God a thing to be grasped, but emptied himself, by taking the form of a servant, being born in the likeness of men. And being found in human form, he humbled himself by becoming obedient to the point of death, even death on a cross.

—Philippians 2:3-8 (ESV)

Relationship-Oriented

And one of the scribes came up and heard them disputing with one another, and seeing that he answered them well, asked him, "Which commandment is the most important of all?"

Jesus answered, "The most important is, 'Hear, O Israel: The Lord our God, the Lord is one. And you shall love the Lord your God with all your heart and with all your soul and with all your mind and with all your strength.' The second is this: 'You shall love your neighbor as yourself.' There is no other commandment greater than these."

—Mark 12:28-31 (ESV)

This is my commandment, that you love one another as I have loved you. Greater love has no one than this, that someone lay down his life for his friends. You are my friends if you do what I command you. No longer do I call you servants, for the servant does not know what his master is doing; but I have called you friends, for all that I have heard from my Father I have made known to you.

—John 15:12-15 (ESV)

Compassionate/Forgiving

Be kind to one another, tenderhearted, forgiving one another, as God in Christ forgave you.

— Ephesians 4:32 (ESV)

For God did not send his Son into the world to condemn the world, but in order that the world might be saved through him.

— John 3:17 (ESV)

Patient / Flexible

The Lord is not slow to fulfill his promise as some count slowness, but is patient toward you, not wishing that any should perish, but that all should reach repentance.

—2 Peter 3:9 (ESV)

Put on then, as God's chosen ones, holy and beloved, compassionate hearts, kindness, humility, meekness, and patience, bearing with one another and, if one has a complaint against another, forgiving each other; as the Lord has forgiven you, so you also must forgive.

—Colossians 3:12-13 (ESV)

Gentle (Not Controlling)

Put on then, as God's chosen ones, holy and beloved, compassionate hearts, kindness, humility, meekness, and patience.

—Colossians 3:12 (ESV)

"Come to me, all who labor and are heavy laden, and I will give you rest. Take my yoke upon you, and learn from me, for I am gentle and lowly in heart, and you will find rest for your souls. For my yoke is easy, and my burden is light."

—Matthew 11:28-30 (ESV)

Grateful

Let the word of Christ dwell in you richly, teaching and admonishing one another in all wisdom, singing psalms and hymns and spiritual songs, with thankfulness in your hearts to God.

—Colossians 3:16 (ESV)

Enter his gates with thanksgiving, and his courts with praise! Give thanks to him; bless his name! For the Lord is good; his steadfast love endures forever, and his faithfulness to all generations.

—Psalm 100:4-5 (ESV)

Free

And you will know the truth, and the truth will set you free.

—John 8:32 (ESV)

I mean that the heir, as long as he is a child, is no different from a slave, though he is the owner of everything, but he is under guardians and managers until the date set by his father. In the same way we also, when we were children, were enslaved to the elementary principles of the world. But when the fullness of time had come, God sent forth his Son, born of woman, born under the law, to redeem those who were under the law, so that we might receive adoption as sons. And because you are sons, God has sent the Spirit of his Son into our hearts, crying, "Abba! Father!" So you are no longer a slave, but a son, and if a son, then an heir through God.

—Galatians 4:1-7 (ESV)

For freedom Christ has set us free; stand firm therefore, and do not submit again to a yoke of slavery.

—Galatians 5:1 (ESV)

Jesus answered them, "Truly, truly, I say to you, everyone who practices sin is a slave to sin. The slave does not remain in the house forever; the son remains forever. So if the Son sets you free, you will be free indeed."

—John 8:34-36 (ESV)

Accepting

Let all bitterness and wrath and anger and clamor and slander be put away from you, along with all malice. Be kind to one another, tenderhearted, forgiving one another, as God in Christ forgave you. Therefore be imitators of God, as beloved children. And walk in love, as Christ loved us and gave himself up for us, a fragrant offering and sacrifice to God.

—Ephesians 4:31-5:2 (ESV)

Now the tax collectors and sinners were all drawing near to hear him. And the Pharisees and the scribes grumbled, saying, "This man receives sinners and eats with them."

—Luke 15:1-2 (ESV)

Factual/Truth-Telling

Therefore, having put away falsehood, let each one of you speak the truth with his neighbor, for we are members one of another.

—Ephesians 4:25 (ESV)

And you will know the truth, and the truth will set you free.

—John 8:32 (ESV)

Healthy Affection

So if there is any encouragement in Christ, any comfort from love, any participation in the Spirit, any affection and sympathy, complete my joy by being of the same mind (with Jesus), having the same love, being in full accord and of one mind (with Jesus).

—Philippians 2:1-2 (ESV)

Greet all the brothers with a holy kiss.

—1 Thessalonians 5:26 (ESV)

Consistent/Predictable

Jesus Christ is the same yesterday and today and forever.

—Hebrews 13:8 (ESV)

"For I the Lord do not change; therefore you, O children of Jacob, are not consumed."

—Malachi 3:6 (ESV)

Rich in Positive Emotions

But the fruit of the Spirit is love, joy, peace, patience, kindness, goodness, faithfulness, gentleness, self-control; against such things there is no law. And those who belong to Christ Jesus have crucified the flesh with its passions and desires.

—Galatians 5:22-24 (ESV)

There are obviously more family characteristics than this brief list. And there are far more Bible references that support each family characteristic than are given here. However, I believe these are the most notable in light of exploring how our families shape us and what God desires. As described in the Bible, God's family relational environment is quite different than most of our families of origin.

In summary, here is a general comparison of an unhealthy, dysfunctional family with a healthy, functional family.

FAMILY ENVIRONMENT COMPARISONS

Unhealthy Family Environment	Healthy Family Environment
Unloving	Loving
Compulsive	Free
Critical	Accepting
Indirect communication	Factual/truth-telling
Inflexible	Patient/flexible
Controlling	Gentle (not controlling)
Ungrateful	Grateful
Non-affectionate	Healthy affection
Distrustful	Trusting
Self-centered	Others-centered
Performance-oriented	Relationship-oriented
Unforgiving	Compassionate/forgiving
Inconsistent	Consistent/predictable
Lacking positive emotions	Rich in positive emotions

This has been a 30,000-foot overview of God's healthy family (the Trinitarian Family). It is important to clarify what a healthy home is before examining our family's relational environment.

Why? Because we must use God's family's relational environment as a standard to compare our family's relational environment to. It is not helpful to compare our homes with our neighbors'. If the majority of our families are dysfunctional, it doesn't help to compare our families to one another. God's family is our only healthy, helpful comparison. With this as our backdrop, we are better able to examine your particular family background.

QUESTIONS

Which three characteristics of the healthy family environment are the most important to you? Why?

_____

_____

_____

_____

Which three characteristics of the healthy family environment do you most struggle to believe can exist? Why?

_____

_____

_____

_____

Which three characteristics of the unhealthy family environment are the most descriptive of your family of origin? Why?

_____

_____

_____

_____

Do you believe that the characteristics of the healthy family environment actually represent the relational environment of the Trinitarian Family? Are these truly the way that God the Father, God the Son, God the Holy Spirit relate to each other and to us?

_____

_____

_____

_____

CHAPTER 6

Understanding Your Family Background

For most of us, starting to pursue real spiritual, emotional, and relational health is like traveling to a distant land. We are told it is there. We've met people who say they have experienced it, but it is still a distant and mysterious place.

Truth be told, it is a journey. And it's well worth the effort. Like any journey, we need to know not only where we are going, but also where we are starting. Every travel plan we make, no matter the destination, has to start from where we are.

Carefully examining our own family backgrounds helps us determine where we are and helps us see where we need to go to become healthy. It's important to understand the undercurrents we personally struggle with from our own background. In doing this, we can more clearly identify the lies and false beliefs that have crept into our thinking about ourselves, God, and life itself.

In this chapter you are going to look at your own specific family background. On the following pages, you will reflect on the relational environment of your family of origin. The questions asked in this chapter may feel intrusive and ominous. It is not always pleasant to revisit the painful memories of your past. However, it is important to briefly go through the pain of looking back to identify events and patterns that shaped you.

If you desire to have God deeply minister to you, you need to allow him access to those deep places where you need his insight and healing. Maybe you resonate with the psalmist when he wrote this:

> Deep calls to deep at the roar of your waterfalls; all your breakers and your waves have gone over me. By day the Lord commands his steadfast love, and at night his song is with me, a prayer to the God of my life. I say to God, my rock: "Why have you forgotten me? Why do I go mourning because of the oppression of the enemy?" As with a deadly wound in my bones, my adversaries taunt me, while they say to me all the day long, "Where is your God?" Why are you cast down, O my soul, and why are you in turmoil within me? Hope in God; for I shall again praise him, my salvation and my God.
>
> —Psalm 42:7-11 (ESV)

Despair and defeat are evident in this passage. The psalmist struggles, wondering why God abandoned him during times he was oppressed or abused. But he is honest with God and himself about the struggles. He goes to the deep places of his soul, "as deep calls to deep." Can you relate to his heartfelt cry and inner-life battle? He deeply wants his inner life and countenance to respond to what his mind knows to be true about God's loving kindness, faithful presence, and care.

The psalmist's emotions seem hijacked by his past experiences, but he does not let this pain stop him from deeply wrestling it through with God.

God desires to go to these deep places of your soul and your darkest pains. God is not the type of surgeon who puts bandages over bullet wounds. Through his skilled, caring hands, he wants to remove the bullets from your festering soul wounds and place his healing salve of loving-kindness and forgiveness on them. In doing so, you will experience some short-term discomfort and pain, but in the long-term you will experience his deep healing.

You may think, "God, do I really need to go back there? I have peace about the events of my past now." We have found that often when Christians say they have peace about traumatic events of their past, they mean they have learned how not to think about them. They have learned the art of preoccupying themselves in such a way they don't have time to think about their pasts. Let us be clear: this is not God's definition of peace!

God's peace comes from his mature perspective and understanding about life events and people. It comes from a renewed mind. Peace means a lack of inner turmoil and struggle; the sea of emotions within you is calm when you think back on your past. You do not need to forget painful people and events of your pasts; your greater need is to understand them in such a way that you can authentically let them go.

True peace is *not* any of the following:

- Forgetting your past problems and troubles

- Satiating yourself or preoccupying your mind so you can't reflect or remember

- Medicating yourself to the point you don't care

You probably know the story of Ebenezer Scrooge. He is the main character in Charles Dickens' 1843 novel *A Christmas Carol*.

Scrooge is a cold-hearted, tight-fisted, selfish man who despises Christmas and all things that engender happiness. The story of his transformation begins with the Ghost of Christmas Past visiting him. The ghost escorts him back to events of his past with the hope of imparting a new perspective on his interactions and relationships. The interactions, conversations, and new perspectives Ebenezer experiences dramatically change his inner life and behavior toward others. His new perspectives transform him.

A similar story is told in the great movie classic *It's A Wonderful Life*. Clarence the angel gives George Bailey a new perspective on his life and the events of his past in a way that is life-changing to him.

We're attempting to bring perspective to your past in a similar way. However, you will not hold the hand of the Ghost of Christmas Past or Clarence, the angel. Instead, I invite and encourage you to hold the hand of your Heavenly Father as you step back. He desires to give you a new perspective concerning your past in a way that results in true peace. Before he can give you a new perspective and understanding, you must first go back there. As you journey, you hold the hand of someone with great strength, wisdom, compassion, and clear perspective—someone you can trust.

As you explore your family background, it's also helpful to reflect on how religious your home environment was. Dysfunction in a home is one kind of pain; dysfunction in a religious home is another. It not only affects how we view ourselves and our relationships, it often affects how we view God.

I encourage you to be honest with yourself and God about your family and the religious experience in your home. Few of us have truly experienced a healthy family environment. This questionnaire is not designed to bash or malign your family. It is meant to look objectively at your experience in your family, to come to terms with how it has impacted you for better or for worse. Take God's hand; go there with him. In the next few chapters, you'll see what new perspectives he wants to give you concerning pains, hurts, and wounds from your past.

FAMILY BACKGROUND QUESTIONNAIRE

Before taking the following questionnaire, it's important to note a few thoughts.

- Please answer the questions in context of your childhood, ages 2 to 18 years of age.

- You are not comparing your home with the average family. Remember, by far, most families are dysfunctional. Answer the questions below comparing your family of origin to the description of the healthy family in chapter 5.

- You are mostly looking for patterns of unhealthy behavior, not just one time events.

- I'm not asking what your perspective is now, or what you now believe looking back at your home of origin. I'm asking you to try to reflect on what you felt as a child. Why? Because what you felt then is what you were responding to as a child, and thus what likely shaped you.

- It will be most helpful if you are honest with yourself about these questions. Pray and ask God to help give you clarity about your childhood. The goal is to reflect on what your home of origin was really like, not exaggerating it as better or worse than it truly was.

1. Did a parent have patterns of struggling with unhealthy inner compulsions that created relational tension in the home? (Examples include overworking, religious obligations, having the house perfectly clean, keeping up with the neighbors, weight loss, etc.)

    ❑ Yes   ❑ No

2. Did you feel there was a pattern of continual relational stress or tension in your home?

    ❑ Yes   ❑ No

3. Was there a pattern of unforgiveness among family members?

    ❑ Yes   ❑ No

4. Was there a parent around whom others had to be careful? (For example: "If _____ ain't happy, ain't nobody happy.")

    ❑ Yes   ❑ No

5. Was there a noticeable absence of regular expressions of love and care (both verbal and nonverbal) toward family members?

    ❑ Yes   ❑ No

6. When there was conflict in your family, especially with a parent, was there a pattern of using one or more of the following during the conflict: blaming, name-calling, yelling, explosive anger, criticism, or ignoring the problem?

    ❑ Yes   ❑ No

7. Did you feel that a parent's love for you or other family members was conditional?

    ❑ Yes   ❑ No

8. Did you or other family members often feel neglected or abandoned?

    ❑ Yes   ❑ No

9. Were displays of strong emotion (that were not manipulative emotion) significantly discouraged in your family? (crying, joy, laughing, sadness, anger, etc.)

    ❑ Yes   ❑ No

10. Did you regularly feel you didn't measure up to a parent's standards in a particular area of your life? (the way you looked physically, in sports, academics, performance of any kind, etc.)

    ❑ Yes   ❑ No

11. Was there a noticeable absence of regular, healthy affection from a parent towards you? (hugs and kisses, hand holding, snuggling, etc.)

    ❑ Yes   ❑ No

12. *Did you fear or experience a physical threat that would bring harm to you by a family member, or did your parents ever physically attack each other in front of you or siblings?

    ❑ Yes   ❑ No

13. *Did a parent have an addiction that affected people relationally in your family? (alcohol, painkillers, drugs, pornography, sports, internet, hunting, fishing, etc.)

    ❑ Yes   ❑ No

14. *Did your parents have a pattern of verbally attacking each other?

    ❑ Yes   ❑ No

15.   **Did a family member ever touch you or have you touch them in a sexual way between the ages of 4-16?

☐ Yes ☐ No

16.   **Did your parents divorce or separate for an extended period of time?

☐ Yes ☐ No

Count the number of questions to which you answered **yes**. Write the total here: _____

Add 3 points for each single * question to which you answered yes: _____

Add 5 points for each double ** question to which you answered yes: _____

Total all three of the above scores: _____

If your total score is:

- 0-3 = You are most likely from a healthy home.

- 4-8 = You are most likely from a confused home. This is a relational environment that has both healthy and unhealthy relational dynamics occurring.

- 8-35 = You are most likely from a stressed or dysfunctional home.

Remember, this is not about blame or shame. This is about the reality of our stories. God already knows our stories and wants us to see them clearly *with* him.

After completing this questionnaire, you may be surprised at what you have discovered about your family of origin. You may have believed your family of origin was healthy, and now after doing this questionnaire you feel doubtful and/or discouraged. If you are feeling discouraged, know you are not alone; most people have not objectively evaluated the relational health of their families of origin. And if you are feeling doubtful, maybe even defensive, try to stay curious and open-hearted about what God may have for you in this exploration. It is completely normal that you may be surprised at your results.

Yes, these family categories do seem subjective. You may wonder how I came up with how many "yes" answers should determine a family's relational health, confusion, or dysfunction. I developed this questionnaire from asking a lot of psychologists, counselors, and therapists their opinions over the last 20 years. I continuously asked, "How much relational dysfunction and pain can happen in a person's childhood before their family environment can be considered dysfunctional or at least confused?" I would also invite you to answer that question for yourself. Most importantly, try to answer in light of God's perspective. Chances are you will also arrive at a similar conclusion to mine.

Now, after taking this questionnaire, what should you do with what you have discovered? Recovery almost always begins with *awareness*. Try your best to become more aware of the relational environments that have shaped you. I pray you will now have more awareness of the inner dynamics that are affecting your current emotional life, behaviors, and relationships. Take note of your tendencies that are shaped by your family background. It's also helpful to know how others you are in close relationship with experience you. Lean into what you need to learn and develop relationally. Use the last few chapters to help you specifically identify what is going on inside you.

If you have found that you were from a healthy home, *celebrate*! You are a part of a small percentage of our population who has experienced what a child should experience. If you discovered you're from a confused or dysfunctional family, you may be seeing this reality for the first time. After watching people go through this process for many years, I can tell you that you are not alone. Many of us thought our family environments were normal or average. And they likely were. Unfortunately, because of the Fall, dysfunction is the norm.

Now, where do you go from here? No matter what your family of origin was like, each family group has things to celebrate and things that need God's healing touch. To grow and heal in Christlikeness, the family groups need each other!

FAMILY GROUPS' STRENGTHS AND WEAKNESSES

It's important to know that every family group has their strengths and weaknesses. God is in the business of redeeming our pasts and using them for His great glory and to build up others. Each family group uniquely shapes and molds certain characteristics into our lives. Some are helpful. Others are not so helpful and need to be addressed. Below are descriptions of what I believe are some of the general strengths and weaknesses of each family group.

Family Group One: Healthy Family Backgrounds

Strengths

The words, pictures, and emotions people in this type of family have about their family background are healthy and consistent with each other. Everything experienced in the family environment matches.

There is no manipulation, deception, or lying because the family is not threatened by what is true. Truth is not used as a relational weapon. Truth is instinctively viewed as protection.

The healthy family runs on trust. They are more likely to take compliments at face value and enjoy them but are not dependent on praise to make their day. They let those compliments pour over their souls.

Every family has conflict. In the healthy family, family members stay in communication with each other until the conflict is resolved and there is reconciliation. They communicate with others to resolve the conflict without using blaming, name-calling, yelling, explosive anger, criticism, or ignoring the problem. They innately understand and can communicate their experiences and memories with authentic emotion.

Weaknesses

Family members sometimes approach the problems of life with platitudes. They have positive healthy emotions, but can often lack real compassion for the hurting and abused of this world, because that world is so foreign to them. They often believe that people who are hurting, if they were not victimized, are hurting because of their own bad choices. They think, "If people would just learn to make better choices, they wouldn't be hurt as much." Real heart-felt empathy tends not to come easily for this family group. As a result, they may lack urgency, along with the courage and confidence in the gospel to change lives.

The word "Lord" may connect more deeply and naturally than with other family groups. The word "Savior" does not always connect deeply with them, because they don't always have a strong felt need for one.

Family Group Two: Confused Family Background

Strengths

Members of confused family backgrounds do have some positive experiences and emotions to build on, and they can feel deeply both the pain and joys of life. They can more easily weep with those who weep, and rejoice with those who rejoice. This family group can relate to the other two family groups in different ways, and because of that they can be a bridge for the other groups to understand one another.

Weaknesses

People from this group tend to instinctively want to earn love. Because of their confused relational past and confused default beliefs, they may mismanage their emotions. They may be inconsistent in relationships because of confused relational skills.

Their ability to trust others will likely come very slowly and be given only after a proven track record in a relationship. They must take time to sort out their family background and to identify what was truly healthy and what was dysfunctional. Because of the confusion about their family background, most likely it will require a second party to help them do this. They starve for compliments but analyze them to the point that they rarely fully enjoy the benefit to their soul.

Family Group Three: Dysfunctional Family Background

Strengths

People from dysfunctional families tend to have an understanding of the deep pain of life, and more often than not, they are not afraid of life. They learn to push through their pain to accomplish what needs to get done, in order to survive. It is out of this family group that we get the most daring and creative Christian leaders. The word "Savior" connects in a deep, meaningful way to them, because they do have a strong felt need for one. They face adversity courageously, because they have faced it all their lives.

Weaknesses

This family group has an inclination not to trust others. Trust for them is just a lower level of suspicion. They tend to instinctively believe it is unwise to trust anyone because that is how a person gets hurt and taken advantage of; they feel it's just a matter of time before someone pulls the rug out from under them. They need to be very intentional to consciously choose to walk by faith (actively trusting God) daily to exchange the lies they have been fed with the truth of God and his deep love and care for them. If they become leaders (either Christian or non-Christian), they may institutionalize their dysfunctions. They have to consciously work against that.

They can greatly struggle with the concept of love. Often, they lack positive emotions. Because it is a struggle for them to trust and sense pure love and loyalty, it is normally a challenge for them to bond in relationships. Frequently, they lack the emotional enzyme needed to digest a compliment, and as a result, they struggle to truly enjoy themselves for who God made them to be.

As you read these family group descriptions, celebrate the strengths you resonate with from your family group. Don't despair over the family group weaknesses you also resonate with. God the Father has something special he wants you to experience in your relationship with him. In your weakness, he is made strong. No matter what your family of origin was like, we are all in great need of recovering from our family background, because God's family is a great improvement on all of our family experiences. His family's relational environment should color our inner life and relationships most.

So how does God recover us from our families of origin? He does so by introducing us and immersing us into his New Family's relational environment.

QUESTIONS

Were there any "aha" moments for you as you completed the family background questionnaire? If so, what were they?

_____

_____

_____

_____

According to the family background questionnaire, which family group do you believe best describes your family of origin: healthy family, confused family, or dysfunctional family?

_____

_____

_____

_____

_____

How accurate is the description of your family background's strengths and weaknesses? Mostly accurate? Mostly inaccurate? Somewhere in the middle? Why?

_____

_____

_____

_____

_____

What questions do you have after reading this chapter?

_____

_____

_____

_____

CHAPTER 7

Recovering From a Hurting Home

RECOVERING FROM AN UNHEALTHY FAMILY BACKGROUND

Maybe you've heard the joke about the Sunday school teacher who asks the children in her class, "What is about the size of a small cat, is gray and furry, has a long bushy tail, and eats nuts?"

Enthusiastically, a young boy raises his hand and says, "Jesus!"

The teacher asks, "Why did you say Jesus?"

The little boy replies, "The right answer in church to any question is always 'Jesus'!"

We chuckle, but in many ways we are no different. If you grew up in the church, you likely *know* that the answer is always Jesus, but sometimes it's hard to make sense of that answer in our daily pain and struggles. We don't understand how a relationship with God touches our brokenness in the here and now. So we want some better advice, a different approach, *something, anything,* to do. The last thing we want is another relationship or a person who might hurt us, use us, or let us down. We just want to finally be fixed. But what if finally being *fixed* means learning what it is to be loved? To be God's beloved? To be in his family?

Let me state it clearly: how God recovers a person from a dysfunctional background is to introduce and adopt them into his New

Family, with a new healthy father (God the Father), new healthy elder brother (Jesus), and a new caregiver (the Holy Spirit). God recovers us through the process of *re-parenting* us. Let's explore this recovery process more carefully.

The Bible speaks of a reality we each should experience in our relationship with God. In Luke 4, Jesus reads about himself from the book of Isaiah:

> "The Spirit of the Lord is upon me, because he has anointed me to proclaim good news to the poor. He has sent me to proclaim liberty (freedom) to the captives and recovering of sight to the blind, to set at liberty those who are oppressed, to proclaim the year of the Lord's favor." And he rolled up the scroll and gave it back to the attendant and sat down. And the eyes of all in the synagogue were fixed on him. And he began to say to them, "Today this Scripture has been fulfilled in your hearing."
>
> —Luke 4:18-21 (ESV)

As you can see from Jesus' words, it is God's intent to do the following:

- Meet those who are in emotional pain
- Rescue those who are brokenhearted
- Minister to those who are from hurting, torn, or abusive relationships
- Bring deep emotional healing as stated in Isaiah

Obviously, God's intent was to fulfill Isaiah's prophecy through Jesus. But it's also clear something is not being effectively understood or integrated into most believers' lives in America.

Just as family and culture have strong influences in our lives, it is God's intention to use a new Heavenly Family to shape us positively with his healthy family characteristics. Regardless of how positive or negative your cultural and family background have been, according to the Bible you are in need of God's influence on your views, on the instinctive pictures you have of yourself, and on who you picture him to be. To effectively integrate these new realities into our lives, God first brings a crisis to our heart's allegiance.

A CRISIS WITHIN CONCERNING OUR FAMILY OF ORIGIN

God brings about a crisis within the hearts and minds of his listeners through the words of Jesus in the New Testament. Read the following verses and note how these words would have brought about an inner crisis and cause anxiety to his listeners, especially because they were a mostly Jewish audience. To the average Jewish person, the family was of great importance. Take note of how his words affect you.

> "Do not think that I have come to bring peace to the earth. I have not come to bring peace, but a sword. For I have come to set a man against his father, and a daughter against her mother, and a daughter-in-law against her mother-in-law. And a person's enemies will be those of his own household. Whoever loves father or mother more than me is not worthy of me, and whoever loves son or daughter more than me is not worthy of me. And whoever does not take his cross and follow me is not worthy of me. Whoever finds his life will lose it, and whoever loses his life for my sake will find it."

> —Matthew 10:34-39 (ESV) (also see Luke 12:51-53)

While he was still speaking to the people, behold, his mother and his brothers stood outside, asking to speak to him. But he replied to the man who told him, "Who is my mother, and who are my brothers?" And stretching out his hand toward his disciples, he said, "Here are my mother and my brothers! For whoever does the will of my Father in heaven is my brother and sister and mother."

—Matthew 12:46-50 (ESV) (also see Mark 3:31-35 and Luke 8:19-21)

"But you are not to be called rabbi, for you have one teacher, and you are all brothers. And call no man your father on earth, for you have one Father, who is in heaven."

—Matthew 23:8-9 (ESV)

Jesus said, "Truly, I say to you, there is no one who has left house or brothers or sisters or mother or father or children or lands, for my sake and for the gospel, who will not receive a hundredfold now in this time, houses and brothers and sisters and mothers and children and lands, with persecutions, and in the age to come eternal life."

—Mark 10:29-30 (ESV)

Now his parents went to Jerusalem every year at the Feast of the Passover. And when he was twelve years old, they went up according to custom. And when the feast was ended, as they were returning, the boy Jesus stayed behind in Jerusalem. His parents did not know it, but supposing him to be in the group they went a day's journey, but then they began to search for him among their relatives and acquaintances, and when they did not find him, they returned to Jerusalem, searching for him. After three days they found him in the temple, sitting among the teachers, listening to them and asking them questions. And all who heard him were amazed at his understanding and his answers. And when his parents saw him, they were astonished. And his mother said to him, "Son, why have you treated us so? Behold, your father and I have been searching for you in great distress." And he said to them, "Why were you looking for me? Did you not know that I must be in my Father's house?" And they did not understand the saying that he spoke to them.

—Luke 2:41-50 (ESV)

And Jesus said to him, "Foxes have holes, and birds of the air have nests, but the Son of Man has nowhere to lay his head." To another he said, "Follow me." But he said, "Lord, let me first go and bury my father." And Jesus said to him, "Leave the dead to bury their own dead. But as for you, go and proclaim the kingdom of God." Yet another said, "I will follow you, Lord, but let me first say farewell to those at my home." Jesus said to him, "No one who puts his hand to the plow and looks back is fit for the kingdom of God."

—Luke 9:58-62 (ESV)

In these passages, Jesus created questions in the minds of his followers:

- Who is Jesus's true family?

- Who is the true family of Jesus's followers?

- To which family do Jesus's followers give their ultimate allegiance and attention?

Jesus's words are strong and intentional. He creates an unmistakable crisis point in our hearts concerning family and our intended Father. Why? In the most effective and heart-moving way possible, Jesus wants to introduce us to our new Father and family. This news is meant to strongly grip our emotions, not just our intellect. By bringing crisis to us emotionally, Jesus is powerfully working to integrate the truths of our New Family into our inner life and into our emotions, where it brings meaningful change.

You and I are being introduced to this New Family in hopes that it will bring lasting change to our hearts. The relational environment of this Heavenly Family is different than our families of origin. The love, care, and providence offered to us through God's family is powerful. Jesus is calling us to a new set of family relationships. Do you hear his beckoning?

QUESTIONS

How do Jesus's words about family and allegiance in this chapter affect you?

_____

_____

_____

_____

What happens in your heart when you read passages like Matthew 10:34-39? Do these words create a crisis in your heart? If so, describe the crisis you are feeling.

_____

_____

_____

_____

How do you feel about God wanting to adopt you into his New Family? Does it make you fearful or excited?

_____

_____

_____

_____

Does it make sense to you that God would use a new relational environment to recover you from a dysfunctional family and world? If so, explain in your own words why this would make sense to you. If not, what questions do you have about it?

_____

_____

_____

_____

CHAPTER 8

Being Re-Parented: Our Need for a New Dad

In the New Testament, Jesus introduces us to our true father, our Father in Heaven. Before Jesus came onto the scene, the people of Israel did not think of God as their father. Only 11 times in the Old Testament is God described like a father. But Jesus not only referred to God as his Father; he announced to his listeners in no uncertain terms that the Holy God of Israel wants to have a relationship with people. In fact, they were to refer to their Holy God as their personal Father.

> "And when you pray, do not heap up empty phrases as the Gentiles do, for they think that they will be heard for their many words. Do not be like them, for your Father knows what you need before you ask him. Pray then like this: "Our Father in heaven, hallowed be your name. Your kingdom come, your will be done, on earth as it is in heaven. Give us this day our daily bread, and forgive us our debts, as we also have forgiven our debtors. And lead us not into temptation, but deliver us from evil."
>
> —Matthew 6:7-13 (ESV)

According to Jesus's teaching on daily prayer, we are to sort out with God on a regular basis these fundamental issues:

- Who is your true Father you look to and listen to in a special way?

- Who or what has your heart's allegiance?

- Are the realities of your heavenly home with him experienced here in your earthly home on a daily basis?

- Are you dependent on him for your most basic daily needs?

- Do you relate to others as your Father relates to you in kindness, mercy, and forgiveness?

- Do you sort out with him your actions and inner-life issues of good (what is of God) and evil (what is of the evil one)?

- Are the realities of your Father's absolute power, authority, and ability an active part of your conscious daily life?

Notice that God likes straight talk. He is not impressed with the extent of our prayers, but is fundamentally interested in the content of our daily conversations with him. Jesus says there are critical issues to be sorted out with God on a daily basis. These issues are fundamental to our inner life and daily relationships. Notice the first issues Jesus said we need to address:

- Who is our real father?

- Where is our heart's allegiance?

Here are some verses where Jesus says your true Father is indeed your Heavenly Father:

- Matthew 5:16

- Matthew 5:45

- Matthew 5:48

- Matthew 6:1

- Matthew 6:14

- Matthew 6:26

- Matthew 6:32

- Matthew 11:25-26

- Luke 11:13

More radical words could hardly have been spoken to the listeners of Jesus's day: children, refer to the Holy God of Israel as your personal Father. It is the first introduction of such a concept. This truth is absolutely critical to a person recovering from a confused or dysfunctional background.

It is God's plan for us to take on a new set of characteristics and instincts from our New Family and our new Father. We are not to react according to our old default beliefs inherited from our culture and family of origin. God is passing on a new set of default beliefs by immersing you into his new, healthy family.

> "But I say to you, Love your enemies and pray for those who persecute you, so that you may be sons of your Father who is in heaven. For he makes his sun rise on the evil and on the good, and sends rain on the just and on the unjust."
>
> —Matthew 5:44-45 (ESV)

For most of us, it is not our instinct to love people who hate us or to pray for those who hurt us. But as we'll see, the New Family environment God the Father brings us into is impacting, power-ful, and life-changing, able to fundamentally rewrite and renew our instincts.

PAUL'S TEACHING CONCERNING GOD AS OUR FATHER

The apostle Paul taught about this important concept of God as our Father as well. Read his words in the following passages. Notice the emphasis on our adoption as children into the New Family and its expensive price: it cost God the Father his first-born Son.

> For all who are led by the Spirit of God are sons of God. For you did not receive the spirit of slavery to fall back into fear, but you have received the Spirit of adoption as sons, by whom we cry, "Abba! Father!" The Spirit himself bears witness with our spirit that we are children of God, and if children, then heirs—heirs of God and fellow heirs with Christ, provided we suffer with him in order that we may also be glorified with him.
>
> —Romans 8:14-17 (ESV)

> But when the fullness of time had come, God sent forth his Son, born of woman, born under the law, to redeem those who were under the law, so that we might receive adoption as sons. And because you are sons, God has sent the Spirit of his Son into our hearts, crying, "Abba! Father!" So you are no longer a slave, but a son, and if a son, then an heir through God.
>
> —Galatians 4:4-7 (ESV)

The word "abba" in the previous verses expresses a very intimate, personal name for father, like our words "papa" or "daddy." Note

Paul's description of the Spirit's work in the inner life of a believer: it results in the heart crying out to God with intimate relationship, "Abba! Father!" or "Daddy!"

> For this reason I bow my knees before the Father, from whom every family in heaven and on earth is named, that according to the riches of his glory he may grant you to be strengthened with power through his Spirit in your inner being. ["Name" meant a person's character, works and reputation, personality, design, and unique qualities.]
>
> —Ephesians 3:14-16 (ESV)

OUR NEED FOR A NEW, HEALTHY PARENT AND FAMILY ENVIRONMENT

In no uncertain terms, God is saying to you that he wants to be your new Father. No matter how wonderful or how painful your experience was with your earthly mother and father, God the Father is saying to us that we are all in great need of being re-parented. This is a fundamental concept, crucial for our full appreciation of God bringing us to internal crisis about our family of origin and introducing himself as our new Father.

God's fatherhood and re-parenting are crucial, because how we view ourselves is essential to receiving our place in the family and its work in our hearts. He knows our self-evaluation, our self-image, is compromised by past interactions with our family of origin and experiences in our culture. When family members and people in our lives relate to us out of their own sin and fallen nature, it presents a fundamental problem.

So, what's the problem? And how does our new, good Father address it?

The Problem With How We Developed Pictures of Ourselves

Here's the crux of the problem: Through thousands upon thousands of interactions with those around us, through both verbal and non-verbal communication, our concepts of "self" have been shaped. People throughout our lives have informed and influenced our understanding of who we are and what we are worth. Most of our identity or self-image shaping occurred from birth to late teens. As mentioned previously, a picture has been painted across your heart of who you are, what makes you worth knowing, and what makes you worthy of relationship. In early life the key identity shapers are likely our father, mother, sisters, and brothers; later on, spouses and even our children play a critical role in identity shaping. Peers, grandparents, stepparents, teachers, pastors, coaches, and other cultural influences also play critical roles in how we view ourselves.

This is an important moment to stop and reflect: *who were the voices in my life and what did they tell me about who I am and what makes me of worth?*

Jesus' words in Luke 14 are key in this discussion:

Now great crowds accompanied him, and he turned and said to them, "If anyone comes to me and does not hate [disregard] his own father and mother and wife and children and brothers and sisters, yes, and even his own life, he cannot be my disciple. Whoever does not bear his own cross and come after me cannot be my disciple."

—Luke 14:25-27 (ESV)

An important note on the word *hate*:

We see the English word "hate" and we think and feel the following:

- Strong feelings of anger
- Revulsion
- Contempt
- Disgust
- Bitterness

This is *not* its meaning in Luke 14:25-27.

The Greek word used in this passage for hate differs immensely from the English definition. It simply means "to strongly disregard." (Strong, 1984)

- There is no emotional tie to anger.
- This disregard is a conscious choice to dismiss others' negative input in light of the truth of who God says we are and what we are worth.
- This disregard is reserved for *critical* and *life-shaping* questions. It is not about what your family thinks; it is about what you accept or believe.

God, in his severe mercy, directly addresses our *key life shapers*. God lists all the people in our lives who typically have the most influence on us. In no uncertain terms, God says he alone desires to be our source of information about life's most critical questions such as these:

- Who am I?
- What am I worth?
- Where is life found?

This only makes sense! God is the only one in our lives who has not stumbled; he is the only one with a perfectly clear view of all things, including each of us. He is saying if we desire to find life, we must die to the old perspectives of ourselves, others, and even God. It's not just dying to old behaviors, but more importantly, dying to those beliefs and perspectives that are the root cause of our sinful behaviors.

This has a sharp edge; don't dull it. The pain and crises brought about from the sharp edge is actually helpful, not hurtful. If you are from a healthy family, these verses can bring clarity and peace to sorting out hidden pain and wounds that happen in every family, no matter how loving. If you are from an unhealthy background, Jesus's words probably sound like freedom! You no longer have to be shaped by the things and people that hurt you; you have a new Father and a New Family!

Jesus says directly and dramatically what he wants you to do:

- Give God exclusive rights to be your deepest influence.

- Put away your fallen concepts about life and yourself. (Die daily to your old self.)

- Walk each moment in the new understanding he gives you about life.

- Walk each moment in the new understanding of who you truly are.

- No longer listen to your fallen family's voice on critical life issues.

- No longer listen to other influences and culture on critical life issues.

- Do not even listen to yourself to define your worth.

Now we listen to and value what God our Father says about us, not the voices of our past.

During the time of Christ, when a person picked up his cross and carried it to where he was to be crucified, his life was already considered over. It was only a matter of time before he physically experienced the reality of what he was experiencing emotionally. The theme of considering our old selves dead is prolific in the New Testament. It's emotive and powerfully impacting for good reason: we need a radical departure from our old approaches to our inner lives and our relationships.

Something dramatic happened next. After Jesus explained this concept, all the tax collectors and sinners drew near to him, and the Pharisees drew away.

> Now the tax collectors and sinners were all drawing near to hear him. And the Pharisees and the scribes grumbled, saying, "This man receives sinners and eats with them."
>
> —Luke 15:1-2 (ESV)

It makes perfect sense that the tax collectors and sinners gathered near to him; they had nothing to lose. They had already been rejected by their families and friends. Finally, someone was reaching out to them in their rejection; they found someone who loved and accepted them for who they were, not what they'd done.

Christ's words were meant for every person, including those who thought their wrongs were not as dreadful as the wrongs of the tax collectors and typical sinners and those who viewed themselves as getting along fine, happy, successful, or good enough.

No one can completely avoid being "stumbled" in some way. No one is surrounded by people with a completely clear view of who they are and what they are worth; God is the only one with that absolutely clear view. Jesus calls every one of us to newly consider what real health and real life with him is.

God wants to paint a new picture of who you are and what you are worth!

QUESTIONS

What does it mean to you personally that God the Father wants to be a dad to you? Do you relate to him in this way? Do you have any fears about interacting with him so relationally?

_____

_____

_____

_____

_____

How does a person hold up God the Father as holy and still relate to him as a personal dad?

_____

_____

_____

_____

_____

Do you see your personal need to be re-parented by God the Father? What specifically in your own life could be addressed by his view of you and his re-parenting?

_____

_____

_____

_____

_____

CHAPTER 9

God the Father's Love for You

GOD THE FATHER'S LOVE AND ACCEPTANCE

Wayne Jacobsen asks in his book *He Loves Me* if any good relationship ever began with a threat. He writes, "No one ever *threatened* to do something that was wonderful." Parents, evangelists, bosses, and others can all achieve some immediate results with threats, but threats do not create or sustain relationships. If we are called to be God's disciples in rich relationship with him, can true trust and love blossom under the grave threat of punishment?

Many of us have come into God's family under threat. Perhaps we responded to the gospel because of a presentation along the lines of "Do it or else you're going to hell." Perhaps it was expected that we follow him because our family made it non-negotiable. We may have hoped the reality of the relationship would eventually be better than "Follow me or else," but so often, we just kept living under the emotional threat that flavored our first meeting with our Father in Heaven. My hope is that you see God the Father as he intended: to see him as your abba. His invitation to you is something that is life-changingly positive.

God is telling us we each need to be re-parented; he wants to be our new Father. In doing so, God wants the exclusive rights to be the one who answers the questions that most deeply influence us.

- Who am I?

- What am I worth?

- Where can I find life?

- What is the purpose of my life?

Like old filthy clothing, he wants us to take off the concepts that we have about life and ourselves and walk about our daily lives in the new understanding that he gives us about life. He wants to fundamentally change who we think we are. This is what it means to die daily to our old selves. No longer are we to listen to the voices of our culture, our fallen families, and other influences concerning critical life issues. Nor are we to listen to self, but we *are* to listen to and *value* what God, our Father, says about us.

> We have to make a definitive choice to
> listen to God, our Father.

We must elevate him above the relationships we have with our earthly fathers, mentors, and leaders. We have to trust him more than any other influence in our hearts and lives.

OUR NEED FOR A GOOD FATHER

No matter our family backgrounds, significant challenges exist for all of us in our perceptions of God. We tend to naively think it is just those from very stressful backgrounds who need to concern themselves with adjusting their view of God the Father and his expectations. In actuality, how we understand our new Father is critically important for everyone.

According to Frank Minirth and Paul Meier, two well-known and respected Christian psychologists, there are five crucial elements for a good self-image from our family of origin, which they explain in their book *Love Is a Choice*:

1. Experiencing unconditional love

2. Clear limits and boundaries; sense of right and wrong

3. Consistency in the home; predictability about daily life

4. An example of how to live

5. A father who is present, interactive, affectionate, and noticeably head of the home

Minirth and Meier report 80 percent of their counselees are clients with a domineering, angry mother and a passive, absent father. If the father was present, he was unaffectionate and was mostly, or inconsistently, passive toward family members. Study interviews conducted with 714 prisoners found two common factors among them:

- Multiple caregivers in their growing up years

- Lack of a stable father figure

This study, among many others, underscores the necessity of a present and compassionate father figure in the home.

Unfortunately for many evangelicals, God the Father is just as vague and absent a father figure as the father in many American homes. The vague picture we carry of God the Father is not God's choice, but rather our lack of biblical understanding.

The challenge before us is to undo the negative effects of our fallen family and cultural background and let our New Family environment do its work. This New Family is just as powerful, or more so, than our family and culture of origin.

To untie the knots caused by years of immersion in an unhealthy or dysfunctional home, we must even more deeply immerse ourselves in our New Family environment. We have to immerse ourselves in such a way that the characteristics of the New Family are not things we just know intellectually, but that we *feel* deeply.

What you feel matters! In brief, emotions don't come out of thin air. Our emotions respond to what we think and believe. If a person does not *feel* truths such as love and joy, at least from time to time, it is evidence that these truths are not actually believed and embraced at a deep, instinctual level. It is *not* failure if you do not experience healthy emotions about God! We are simply making the correlation here that our emotions reflect on the outside what we think and believe deep within.

An important note on God's holiness:

We want to make clear that though we are discussing God the Father's unconditional love and acceptance, we are doing this in the context of his holiness. We believe it is critically important to understand that we are talking about the Holy God of the Bible. God the Father is all of these:

- The God of the Old and New Testament

- The mighty, all-powerful, all-knowing God who spoke the stars, the earth, and all of creation into being

- The Holy God of Israel

As we experience God, his holiness does not contradict or diminish his love for us. In fact, God's holiness makes his love and goodness toward us as a father even more profound.

OUR NEW FATHER'S FAMILY VALUES

As Christians, we have been adopted into a New Family in a very real way. What can we learn about adoption from non-infant children who are welcomed into a new home? For a non-infant child to successfully be brought into a new family environment, several things need to be experienced. Adopted children need to know and feel the following:

- They belong and are safe and secure in their new family.

- They are wanted and valued by their new parents.

- They are just as valuable as existing family members.

- They have time to adjust to their new family values and relational environment.

As you read the following words from Isaiah about the Coming Messiah, fulfilled by Jesus, keep these things in mind and notice what your new Father has done and said to make you feel wanted, valuable, and secure in the New Family environment into which you are adopted. Also, pay attention to the pronouns used in this passage. There are several persons being referred to: Jesus, God the Father, and those of us who have been redeemed by Christ's sacrifice.

> Surely our griefs He Himself [Jesus] bore,
> And our sorrows He [Jesus] carried;
> Yet we ourselves esteemed Him [Jesus] stricken,
> Smitten of God, and afflicted.
> But He [Jesus] was pierced through for our transgressions,
> He [Jesus] was crushed for our iniquities;
> The chastening for our well-being fell upon Him [Jesus],
> And by His [Jesus's] scourging we are healed.
> All of us like sheep have gone astray,

Each of us has turned to his own way;
But the Lord [God the Father] has caused the iniquity
of us all
To fall on Him [Jesus].
He [Jesus] was oppressed and He [Jesus] was afflicted,
Yet He [Jesus] did not open His [Jesus's] mouth;
Like a lamb that is led to slaughter,
And like a sheep that is silent before its shearers,
So He [Jesus] did not open His [Jesus's] mouth.
By oppression and judgment He [Jesus] was
taken away . . .
His [Jesus's] grave was assigned with wicked men,
Yet He [Jesus] was with a rich man in His [Jesus] death,
Because He [Jesus] had done no violence,
Nor was there any deceit in His [Jesus's] mouth.
But the Lord [God the Father] was pleased
To crush Him [Jesus], putting Him [Jesus] to grief;
If He [Jesus] would render Himself as a guilt offering,
He [God the Father] will see His offspring [Jesus],
He [God the Father] will prolong His [Jesus's] days,
And the good pleasure of the Lord [God the Father]
will prosper in His [Jesus's] hand.
As a result of the anguish of His [Jesus's] soul,
He [God the Father] will see it and be satisfied;
By His [Jesus's] knowledge the Righteous One,
My Servant [Jesus], will justify the many,
As He [Jesus] will bear their iniquities.
Therefore, I [God the Father] will allot Him [Jesus] a
portion with the great,
And He [Jesus] will divide the booty with the strong;
Because He [Jesus] poured out Himself to death,

And was numbered with the transgressors;
Yet He Himself [Jesus] bore the sin of many,
And interceded for the transgressors.

—Isaiah 53:4-12 (NASB 1995)

The sacrificial acts God has done for our well-being are striking. Notice Isaiah 53:6, "All of us like sheep have gone astray, Each of us has turned to his own way." In spite of our condition and our relational passivity and rebellion toward him, God the Father sacrificially gave his own Son on our behalf.

Listen to the words describing what his Son went through on our behalf:

- Jesus was *crushed*.

- Jesus was *oppressed*.

- Jesus was *afflicted*.

- Jesus will *bear their iniquities*; our sin and wrongdoing fell upon him.

- His soul was *anguished*.

- By his *scourging* we are healed.

Jesus' mode of operation was not like our culture, in which we avoid pain and seek comfort. There is not a sense of self-entitlement within the family circle of the Trinity. God obviously has a higher relational goal. His goal was to redeem the lost at great expense. Notice God the Father's response to what he was watching his Son go through; the descriptions are staggering:

"But the Lord was pleased to crush Him, putting Him to grief."

"He will see it [His only Son being crushed] and be satisfied."

The Hebrew word for "satisfied" expresses a type of satisfaction that gives you a deep sense of pleasure. (Strong, 1984) Those of us who are parents probably can't imagine being able to stand watching our children suffer, especially if they were innocent, suffering for the wrongdoing of someone else.

But God the Father said he was pleased to crush his Son. It was deeply satisfying to him because of what this sacrificial act would accomplish.

His Son was put through this grief in order to be an offering for us. Jesus bore our iniquities and sin so we might enter into a relationship with the Trinity. Jesus willingly accepted death for us, since he knew the relational gain it would bring. This was the cost of the adoption process. A good father aggressively pursued his lost children. He spared no expense to accomplish his desire. God's deep character quality of justice had to be satisfied. The only one who was innocent and could take on the penalty of the wrongdoing of others was his innocent Son.

In one act, God's justice and love was satisfied. What an incredible love! What an incredible act! This passage is humbling. It reveals the value God the Father has for fallen, lost, undeserving children like you and me. This passage begins to reveal a family value system that is quite foreign to us. But it doesn't end here.

Many of our homes were—or are—more like war zones than sanctuaries. The trauma experienced in many of our families is as great as if we were in the midst of a war zone. People within these families often believe and communicate, "What you have done has far more significance than who you are." This broken value system says, "Forget who you are! Because of what you have done, I reject your person and I dislike you."

God's family does not work that way. The scriptures make it very clear that God our Father is more preoccupied with the person than what the person has done. This is the great biblical truth that should have a tremendous psychological effect on the Christian. God has already solved the issue of sin and wrongdoing. Jesus died for every sin and wrongdoing. He wiped them away. Only the significance of the child of God remains.

WHAT ARE THE VALUES OF OUR NEW HEAVENLY FAMILY?

Values help us define the qualities and principles we believe are most important. A person's values tell us what they most esteem and desire. Values speak to both our minds and our hearts.

The apostle Paul's words in Romans 5 show us a great deal about our New Family values. What do your intellect and emotions experience as you read this scripture about God's value system?

> Therefore, having been justified by faith [active trust], we have peace with God through our Lord Jesus Christ, through whom also we have obtained our introduction by faith into this grace in which we stand; and we exult in hope of the glory of God. And not only this, but we also exult [visible joy] in our tribulations [life's daily trials], knowing that tribulation brings about perseverance; and perseverance, proven character; and proven character, hope; and hope does not disappoint, because the love of God has been poured out within our hearts through the Holy Spirit who was given to us. For while we were still helpless, at the right [strategic] time Christ died for the ungodly. For one will hardly die for a righteous man; though perhaps for the good man someone would dare

even to die. But God demonstrates His own love toward us, in that while we were yet sinners, Christ died for us.

—Romans 5:1-8 (NASB 1995)

OUR NEW FAMILY VALUE OF TRUST

Most of us are still learning what trust is. We are also learning the value of trust. This is a challenge if you grew up in a home haunted by compulsive behavior such as alcoholism or addiction, where every word you heard became tainted by the dysfunctional atmosphere of the family. Every kind word was contradicted by the emotional and behavioral environment.

When you grow up in a family that runs on shame, where people are controlling and inflexible as well as critical and ungrateful, mistrust becomes the norm. Deep, irrational suspicion becomes part of the air we breathe. The level of distrust is so high that the very idea of trust is incomprehensible.

If you are from an unhealthy background, you'll begin to embrace the idea that love can get you hurt, and trust can get you killed. The word trust can take on new meaning. Trust may mean that you can count on a person to be reliable once in a while. Trust becomes, in fact, simply a lower level of suspicion. This kind of "trust" is the only kind many people have come to know, because it's all they have experienced. They have never experienced the affectionate consistency of another loving person. But "occasional reliability" is not the biblical definition of trust. If a person's family background is unhealthy, growth toward real trust is important.

Can you have any type of meaningful relationship without trust? No! It's fundamental to all relationships. You cannot even have a business relationship with someone without trusting them. Trust allows us to give someone access to our heart. Without trust, others remain at arms-length from us. We can be with others 24/7, eat with them, sleep with them, have sex with them, share a bank account, and much more, but if we don't trust them, we feel alone— and we are.

Why is trust so vital to daily life? Trust is the relational vehicle that allows family members to be actively involved in each other's lives.

Trust is one of the highest values in a healthy family, enabling family members to know exactly what is going on in each other's lives. This openness about what is going on with people gives opportunity to celebrate life's daily joys, to intervene when help is needed, and to comfort when pain and hurt are present. Trust is the pathway to true relationship and intimacy. When there is no trust, there is no relationship. The depth of any relationship directly correlates to the amount of trust extended. Life's daily conscious choices are connected to trust. Trust drives right to the heart, determining almost every functional and relational response we make on a daily basis.

Trust is one of the most important values in Christianity and one of the most powerful psychological forces behind relationships in the family of God. The Trinity operates on trust. God's desire for his family is that we trust each other every day and every second. Trust is the very air we are to breathe. For many of us, this is a totally foreign atmosphere.

It's because of this that God has made trust one of the most important family values within His Heavenly Family. Trust is the very first thing Paul speaks to: faith. Faith is just another way of saying—and practicing—active trust in something not visibly seen. The first value to which we are introduced is faith, so that we would show complete "active trust" in the grace—literally, "an undeserved gift"—we continually stand in as believers. One of the highest values our New Family operates by is active trust. Trust (faith) is central to God's family.

OUR NEW FAMILY VALUE OF PROVEN CHARACTER

Another value of note in this passage is proven character. Tribulations, our life's problems, now have a purpose and are of great value to us. In our New Family's value system, our problems produce in us something of precious worth: proven character. Tribulations are no longer random acts of pain. Daily problems and seemingly over-whelming life struggles now produce character that is highly valued in God's family.

This new character points back to a good God who pours his love into our hearts. We have a character that reflects hope even when we are in ashes. Make no mistake about it: this is a New Family value. Pain from struggles is not normally viewed in our culture as something in which we rejoice, but this view is short-sighted. Our new Father teaches us that our tribulations can actually produce in us something that is of relational value. When life gets hard, we all want to be surrounded by people with proven character. You may have heard the old saying "When the going gets tough, the tough get going." For many of us, because of our family backgrounds, we hear this saying differently. When things got tough, the "not so tough" got going, meaning they simply took off, got out of town, split the scene. People who have character, who've learned to endure hardship, are not likely to abandon their families when things get tough. God is not the only one who values character—we all do.

OUR NEW FAMILY VALUE OF HOPE

We are introduced to another New Family characteristic: hope. This is hope that does not disappoint us. The Greek word for "disappoint" can better be translated as "shame," to hide or cower in fear. We no longer have to be ashamed of our problems; those problems are now of great worth and are producing something of incredible value.

Many place their hope in people, ways of life, and things that eventually deeply disappoint them. Often, people are ashamed of where, how, and in what they placed their hope. But for the children of God, our trust is not misplaced and our hope is not empty. We no longer have to hide in shame from God and others, because we have found a good Father in God, and we now have peace with him.

The children of God should have a very important psychological dynamic going on deep within them: hope! Hope is very important when it comes to enduring pain, being patient, and having the ability to look outside yourself during difficult times. As children of our good Father, we now know there is something beyond our daily problems and struggles.

According to the Romans 5 passage, we can know this hope because God has poured out his love for us through the Holy Spirit into our hearts. We can know that we are greatly loved and cared for by our new Father.

God provides a constant, tangible reminder to us that we are greatly loved and can trust in our New Family environment: the cross!

For while we were still helpless, at the right time Christ died for the ungodly. For one will hardly die for a righteous man; though perhaps for the good man someone would dare even to die. But God demonstrates his own love toward us, in that while we were yet sinners, Christ died for us.

—Romans 5:6-8 (NASB 1995)

It is critical to note *when* God chose to give his Son for us: he said it was at the "right time."

In the original Greek, two words could have been used here. Paul could have used "chronos" (Strong, 1984, #5550), which means a specific time of the day, according to the position of the sun or the time on a clock. We get our word "chronological" from this word. The other word used to indicate time is "kairos" (Strong, 1984, #2540), meaning a strategic time. Kairos expresses the idea of when the time was right, when the right things were happening, or when it was the strategic time. The word Paul used was kairos, the strategic time.

It was not when we were at our best that God the Father gave his Son for us. The strategic time was not when we were in our strength or when we were most "godly." The strategic time God gave his Son for us was when we were continually helpless and ungodly. God the Father demonstrated his own particular type of love for us in that while we were continually sinning (being passive, indifferent, and rebellious towards him), Christ died for us. The strategic time he chose to give his own Son was when we were at our worst. It is the cross that is our constant reminder of our hope and of God's particular type of love for us.

It is because of this type of love poured into our hearts that we can come out of hiding, out of our shame, and into life with a daily, unwavering hope. This is unmistakable evidence that God the Father values persons over what they do. God the Father is preoccupied with you, not with what you have done or not done. In an unhealthy home, what you have done has far more significance than who you are. That is not how our New Family operates. We value people over their daily mistakes and bad decision-making. This is one of the characteristics of a healthy family.

Here is what we have learned from Romans 5:

- We have been introduced to a family who actively trusts each other.

- Our daily problems now have a redemptive purpose: they build our character.

- We no longer have to hide in shame; we can come out into the open because of love.

- God chose a very strategic time to show us how much he loves us—when we were at our worst.

OUR NEW FAMILY VALUE OF BEING OF GREAT WORTH

In order for us to step toward health when we come from a dysfunctional family background or an unhealthy culture, key questions need to be answered:

- Who am I?

- What am I worth?

- Where can I find life?

- What is the purpose of my life?

In Romans 5:1-8, the answers to many of these questions are addressed. The issue of trust does not come from a concept or a religion, but from the persons of the Trinity—persons who place a high value on trust. In our New Family, active trust is one of the most important aspects of family life. We find a healthy family with a Father who can turn our daily struggles into something that produces the character God and our New Family value.

We also see in Romans 5 that he is not a passive, absent, or unloving father. He moved toward us even while we were being passive, indifferent, and rebellious toward him. God the Father offered us the strongest expression of love by giving his only begotten Son to satisfy his good character qualities of both justice and love. A healthy father can now be found in our Heavenly Father who gave the unimaginable to bring us into his family. Our new healthy Father has done everything to earn our trust.

THE IMPORTANCE OF WORTH

A sense of worth is hard to develop in an unhealthy or dysfunctional home. Too often family members are fighting sadness and depression. Family members communicate to each other out of their own painful moods, not considering that they are shaping someone else's sense of identity and worth.

Our sense of worth, either positive or negative, is a powerful force in our lives, as authors Lynch, McNicol, and Thrall explain in their book *The Cure*. It's the deep sense of a lack of self-worth that keeps the prostitute in business, the runaway child from going home, or the addict from considering the possibility of quitting something he knows will eventually kill him. If you believe you are equal to a piece of dirt, it is not hard at all to do dirty things. If you believe the worth of a child or another person is equal to a bug, it is not at all a stretch to mistreat that child or person.

Statements made in our childhoods that help shape this low sense of worth start with words like "You're nothing but a . . ." These kinds of statements may not be communicated just through words, but through neglect or a lack of attention. You may have sensed that you were not someone worthy of attention or with whom to spend time. You may have been mistreated in a way that said you were only worthy of abuse, disgust, and ridicule. Actions almost always speak more loudly than words.

> If we conclude we are of no real worth, we can easily project that feeling onto others.

How can the worth of a person be determined? Can it be correlated with the amount of money you are worth? Is it according to the grades you got in school? Are you valuable because of your achievements, your outward appearance, your career, your usefulness to society, or the attention you get from the opposite sex? The problem with using any of these perspectives to measure your worth is that all of these things can fluctuate with time, due to any number of factors. To feel good about yourself or have a great sense of self-worth, you would always have to achieve highly, or stay healthy, or not gain weight, or be on your "A" game. A simple observation of the men and women who have gone before us quickly reveals that accidents happen, weight gain and disease happen, the economy changes, and wrinkles are a natural part of growing older.

Have you ever wondered what would happen if you were kidnapped? If kidnappers sent a note to your closest relatives demanding a large ransom, what would your relatives be willing to pay to get you back? How much would they sacrifice for you?

People from every walk of life, the rich and poor, the highly successful and seemingly ruined, the beautiful and unlovely, the popular and unnoticed, all struggle with feelings of their own worthlessness.

WHAT ARE YOU WORTH?

How does God the Father answer this question?

God says in Romans 5 that *you are worth a Son to him*. When your own family and friends wouldn't take out a second mortgage on their homes to save your skin, God your Father, a truly good Father, gave his only begotten, innocent Holy Son for you. Take a minute and stop to feel the emotion that this thought brings you.

The question of how you should view yourself is also effectively addressed in Romans 5. You are not an accumulation of your daily problems. You are not what you do. You need not be preoccupied any longer with what you do to define your worth; your New Family is preoccupied with who you are to them, not with what you have done. A part of the answer of who you are is now answered by our good Father. He says that you are a very valuable son or daughter of the most High God. Who you are is a valued child that he gave everything for. He gave his own Son to rescue you.

God the Father is more preoccupied with you, not what you have done!

We must be intentional and vigilant to continually see ourselves in light of theological truths. The images and pictures the Bible informs us about are vitally important to our psyche. We must replace our old image of what a father is with the new one God is supplying for us. We don't think in words alone; words create concepts and pictures in our minds. They are ultimately the pictures to which our hearts respond. They shape how our inner lives develop. We must fight to replace our old family images we equate with father, love, trust, etc. with pictures from our New Family with God the Father.

GOD'S LOVE AND ACCEPTANCE IS FOUNDATIONAL

God makes clear in Ephesians 3 that his love for and acceptance of us is to be the very foundation of our inner life or psyche:

> For this reason I bow my knees before the Father, from whom every family in heaven and on earth is named, that according to the riches of his glory he may grant you to be strengthened with power through his Spirit in your inner being, so that Christ may dwell in your hearts through faith—that you, being rooted and grounded in love, may have strength to comprehend with all the saints what is the breadth and length and height and depth, and to know [experientially] the love of Christ that surpasses knowledge, that you may be filled with all the fullness of God.
>
> **—Ephesians 3:14-19 (ESV)**

The Greek word for heart is "cardia." In *The New Testament: An Expanded Translation*, Kenneth Wuest defines cardia as the place where what we know meets that which we feel deeply. Your heart is not simply what you know, nor is it simply what you feel. It is the place within you where you feel deeply about what you are thinking. For example, when someone is emotional about a topic as they speak, we say they are "sharing from their heart." In other words, they feel deeply about the ideas they are sharing. This expression is consistent with the New Testament use of the word cardia.

The apostle Paul said the very foundation from which a Christian should live is a deeply rooted and grounded sense of being loved and accepted by God the Father. These senses are both deeply psychological and emotional.

Unfortunately for many, Christianity has become a horrible textbook religion. It has become so overly intellectualized. We have substituted the childlike, trusting acceptance of being liked and loved by God the Father with an abstract, intellectual understanding of God's love.

These scriptures are not just a list of cold, hard facts that we read as from a dictionary. This is a passionate love letter, from a passionate God, to his deeply loved and newly adopted children. From these verses, God strongly communicates the importance of his own particular type of love as the very foundation of our psychological and emotional makeup.

If the foundation of a building or house is not deep enough, or if it is built with the wrong material, the building will eventually fall apart. God is communicating in no uncertain terms that the foundation of a person's inner life must be built on a firm and deep understanding of his love. The goal is not that we would have a solely intellectual knowledge of God's love.

The word used for "to know" in Ephesians 3, verse 19, is the word "ginosko" (Strong, 1984, #1097). This type of knowledge is experiential. The goal is not just to hear about God's love but to experience it firsthand. His love should be something that we personally *experience* in our daily lives.

WE HAVE A GREAT NEED TO PERSONALLY, DEEPLY DIGEST HIS LOVE

Make Paul's prayer for the believers in Ephesus the prayer of your heart.

> I do not cease to give thanks for you, remembering you in my prayers, that the God of our Lord Jesus Christ, the Father of glory, may give you the Spirit of wisdom and of revelation in the knowledge of him, having the eyes of your hearts enlightened, that you may know what is the hope to which he has called you, what are the riches of his glorious inheritance in the saints.
>
> —Ephesians 1:16-18 (ESV)

Again, note the word for heart here is cardia—the place where what we know meets the thoughts or things about which we feel deeply. Paul prayed God would give people in the churches throughout Asia Minor a revelation: knowledge about God's thoughts, which would deeply affect them mentally and emotionally. He prayed the eyes of their hearts (remember that eyes in Scripture usually refers to perspective) would be enlightened. He prayed they would see something that would cause a new understanding. Paul prayed his readers would see something and as a result would feel deeply about it.

What did Paul pray these believers would see?

- The hope of this new calling (as adopted children of God).

- That this hope is the riches of the glory (the revealed greatness) of God the Father's inheritance in the saints (the children of God).

In other words, Paul prays we would see how precious an inheritance God the Father is receiving in his relationship with us; he longs for us to experience how much the Father loves us. Many will misread this passage and think that what the eyes of our hearts need to see is the inheritance *we* are receiving from God. It is not our inheritance that we are to see; it is God's inheritance in us that Paul wants us to see. Of all the things Paul chose to pray for these people at Ephesus (and for us), Paul chose to pray that we would see how deeply precious we are to God the Father. We have a need for our perspective to change concerning God's love for us.

THE EFFECT OF A RELATIONSHIP WITH GOD THE FATHER ON YOUR INNER LIFE

It is an American cultural norm to seek answers to our inner-life pain through pills, hypnosis, or any number of distractions. Contrary to our culture, the Bible says the cure to what ails us is found in relationship.

If you think about it, most of the woes of our inner lives are caused by hurtful or non-existent relationships. It stands to reason that if unhealthy relationships cause most of our inner turmoil, then the likely solution would be a healthy relationship. This was Jesus's answer. He said the answer to the anxiety that plagues us is a loving, trust-based relationship with a new Father. The answer to anxiety is not working harder, taking more pills, or seeing a psychiatrist; the answer is a relationship with a Heavenly Father who cares for you. (To clarify, appropriate use of medications and professional help are often important treatments for anxiety. However, they don't remove the need for a relationship with God.)

> "Therefore do not be anxious, saying, 'What shall we eat?' or 'What shall we drink?' or 'What shall we wear?' For the Gentiles seek after all these things, and your heav-

enly Father knows that you need them all. But seek first the kingdom of God and his righteousness, and all these things will be added to you. Therefore do not be anxious about tomorrow, for tomorrow will be anxious for itself. Sufficient for the day is its own trouble."

—Matthew 6:31-34 (ESV)

Some words to pay special attention to are words like "But seek first." Jesus said the first step in dealing with inner life issues like anxiety is to seek after the Heavenly Father. Other critical words are "his Kingdom and his righteousness." This refers to the ways God the Father manages his Kingdom and those within it. Of course, if a person thought God the Father managed his household and behaved like their earthly father, many of us would have reason for anxiety. That's why this issue of God the Father is so critical. It is imperative that we see him as the Father that he truly is. He is not absent, distant, or uncaring. He is ever watching over us and looking for opportunities to reveal himself as a caring Father.

Jesus pleads with us to see God as the type of father he truly is:

"Ask, and it will be given to you; seek, and you will find; knock, and it will be opened to you. For everyone who asks receives, and he who seeks finds, and to him who knocks it will be opened. Or what man is there among you who, when his son asks for a loaf, will give him a stone? Or if he asks for a fish, he will not give him a snake, will he? If you then, being evil, know how to give good gifts to your children, how much more will your Father who is in heaven give what is good to those who ask Him!"

—Matthew 7:7-11 (NASB 1995)

Jesus says in the clearest way that God the Father is a drastic improvement over even the best human fathers. He portrays God as someone waiting for an opportunity to reveal himself. It's interesting that he uses a comparison of the ways of earthly fathers with the ways of God the Father. He acknowledges that all earthly fathers have an inherent problem of being "evil."

God the Father is above the influence of moods and actions caused by sin and its effects on an earthly father's actions. Even the best of Christian and non-Christian fathers fall prey to their changing moods and emotions. Yet, even being susceptible to a bad mood occasionally, most fathers still would not deceive or mistreat their child who asks for something they need.

Our Heavenly Father never falls prey to sinful moods and emotions. His ways as a Father are unchanging, predictable, and full of love and grace. Who you are as his son or daughter is far more important than what you have done. His kingly ways and righteousness are based on his being more preoccupied with you as a person and his relationship with you than with what you have done. If you are uncertain about this, Jesus's plea with you is to ask, seek, and knock on his door. He says to *seek first* God the Father and how he goes about his parenting and rule. If you do this, your inner life is going to respond to his good parenting.

GOD THE FATHER'S LOVE AND THE THREE FAMILY GROUPS

The Importance of Our New Father

Because of our unhealthy backgrounds, we each have unique obstacles to truly seeing with our hearts who God the Father is and what he has done for us. Let's explore the challenges each family background faces as they begin to relate healthfully with our new Heavenly Father and experience his love and care.

To Those From a Healthy Home

The terms *healthy*, *confused*, and *dysfunctional* are, of course, relative. A healthy family is not a perfect family. If you are from a healthy family background, you likely grew up with some predictable characteristics people from other family backgrounds did not enjoy. Some of your experience may have included the following:

- A home of genuine affection binding the family together

- The family genuinely liked each other and you probably like yourself

- An emotional environment richly communicating safety and wellness

However, your challenge is to realize that Jesus knew people from healthy families still have a strong, real need for God the Father. Jesus assumes the healthiest parent has sin and a level of maliciousness in their life. This may not be a comfortable truth. It's easy to compare ourselves to others and walk away feeling better; however, when we compare ourselves to how God looks at reality, we do not fare as well.

God the Father has higher hopes that transcend any background: his desire is for you to live according to the practice of the Heavenly Family. Your Heavenly Father wants more than just love within the home for one another; he wants the presence of a greater and wider love. Frequently in our research and interviews, we note that people from healthy homes (whether Christian or not) lack empathy for those outside the family circle, especially for those who appear to be trapped by their family background. Jesus directly challenged that mindset, saying the love within the home should be extended to those outside the home and to those who are undesirable.

When you became a Christian, you entered more than just another healthy family. Whether you are from a thoroughly dysfunctional background or the healthiest family on the planet, joining the Father's trinitarian family is an incredible improvement over any situation.

There is no room for self-righteousness with God. You need him desperately! Jesus asks you in Matthew 7 to see this. Ultimately, you are descended from Adam's family; sin runs through your spiritual veins just as deeply as in those who are from the darkest of family backgrounds. Run to your new Father and enjoy in a deeper way what you have seen here as a foreshadowing of your heavenly home!

To Those From a Confused Home

If you are from a confused family background, you likely existed in a barter system. Growing up, you may have learned to trade parent-pleasing behavior for affection, love, grace, and acceptance. In God's Family system, love is never based on your actions; it is based on who you are.

Again, God our Father is more preoccupied with you as a person than with what you have done. Your challenge is to gain an accurate perspective in order to see a true picture of God's love. Accurate images are vitally important for you; ultimately, these images are what move your heart to respond.

Replace the old images of family members who are keeping score of all the rights and wrongs with a Father who—even in the midst of your worst failures—looks at you with deep delight and acceptance!

To Those From a Dysfunctional Home

If you are from an unhealthy background, as an adult you may have frequently found yourself in one of these circumstances:

- Emotionally shut down

- Medicating your inner life pain

- Abused by those closest to you

- Afraid of relationships

- Suspicious

- Betrayed by parents or spouse

- Tending to preoccupy yourself with addictive behaviors

Life experiences may have led to fear, anger, confusion, and sadness dominating your daily emotions. You need exactly what our Heavenly Father offers: a healthy New Family life.

Your New Family is a more powerful, life-shaping force than your dysfunctional family of origin; the New Family exists to influence and shape your inner life. You must deeply immerse yourself into your New Family environment.

Immerse yourself in these heavenly truths, not just intellectually, but experientially. Allow God to take these truths as deep as your deepest pain. Push them as deep as your suspicions go. Replace the images attributed to untrue, inaccurate words and voices from your old family background (father, love, trust, etc.) with new images and pictures from our New Family with God the Father. Receive it deeply: you are worth a Son to him!

IMMERSE YOURSELF IN GOD THE FATHER'S LOVE AND ACCEPTANCE

God the Father says these things about himself:

- I am the great I Am. (Exodus 3:14)

- I am God the Father from whom are all things. (Corinthians 8:6)

- All of creation came from my mind and heart. (Genesis 1:1-2:25)

- I am full of mercy, grace, and unfailing love. (Psalm 86:15)

- You were made in my image, inwardly and outwardly. (Genesis 1:27)

- I am your *Father*; I have declared you *my child*. (1 John 3:1)

- I know everything about you. (Psalm 139:1)

- I am familiar with all your ways. (Psalm 139:3)

- Not even a hair drops from your head that I don't know about. (Matthew 10:29-31)

- Consider me and call me your Abba, Daddy—your Papa. (Romans 8:15)

- I am a father who gives good gifts perfectly designed for you. (Matthew 7:11)

- Rather than being distant and angry, I am the complete expression of love. (1 John 4:16)

- A nursing mother can forget her children, but I will NEVER forget you. (Isaiah 49:15)

- You are my treasured possession. (Exodus 19:5)

- I am your greatest encourager. (2 Thessalonians 2:16-17)

- I lavish you with my love and delight. (1 John 3:1)

- I lavish you with my grace. (Ephesians 1:7-8)

- I love you with an everlasting love. (Jeremiah 31:3)

- I rejoice over you with singing. (Zephaniah 3:17)

- I am sometimes speechless in my love for you. (Zephaniah 3:17)

- I dance over you with shouts of pure joy. (Zephaniah 3:17)

- I will *never, ever* leave or forsake you, period. (Hebrews 13:5, John 14:18)

- I demonstrated my love for you by giving my only begotten Son. (Romans 5:8)

- Even when you lose your faith (active trust) in me, I will never lose my faith (active trust) in you. (2 Tim. 2:13)

- I delight in you even as I delight in my Son, Jesus. (John 17:23)

- You are invaluable to me: worth the death of my Holy Son. (Romans 5:6-8)

- Make my love your abiding and comfortable home. (John 15:9, 1 John 4:16)

- When you were at your worst, I strategically chose that very moment to demonstrate my delight in you. (Romans 5:6-8)

- *Nothing* can separate you from my love. (Romans 8:35-3)

QUESTIONS

What would shift in you—become different in you—if you were well-loved during your developmental years? A family like the following:

- A family where Mom and Dad affirmed and delighted in you

- A family in which you were fully accepted as-is

- A family that was extremely affectionate

- A family where trusting one another was the norm

- A family that was thrilled to see you each day

_____

_____

_____

_____

_____

What if this was the kind of family you were in now? One where the norm was abundant and generous love, delight in one another, a lot of warm affection, plentiful patience, unconditional acceptance, nonthreatening honesty, and no chance of ever being abandoned. How would being part of this kind of family change you? (If you are a believer, you are being invited into a relational environment just like this through the Trinitarian Family. The description you gave of how this family would change you can be true!)

_____

_____

_____

_____

_____

What specifically did you need from your dad (or dads, depending on your own story) that you did not receive but would have changed your life in a positive way? What specifically did you need from your dad(s) that you *did* receive?

_____

_____

_____

_____

_____

What did you need from your mom (or moms, depending on your own story) that you did not receive but would have changed your life in a positive way? What specifically did you need from your mom(s) that you *did* receive?

_____

_____

_____

_____

_____

CHAPTER 10

God the Son's Love for You

We have looked closely at our new Father and his role in our New Family environment. Now, we'll look more closely at Jesus, the elder brother of our New Family, and his unique role.

JESUS'S LOVE AND SACRIFICE

According to the Bible, Jesus is the older brother of the family of God. Romans 8:29 says, *"that he [Jesus] might be the first-born among many brothers."* Being the older brother, Jesus willingly took upon himself the responsibility to pay the penalty for our sin so we could be adopted into the family of God.

From the beginning of the fall of man, God spoke of one who would come to redeem man and help restore mankind to himself. The prophets spoke of the one who would come to take upon himself the rightful punishment of man's sin. Specific prophecies were made about this Messiah (the Anointed One), so we could know him when he emerged. Jesus Christ is the subject of more than 300 Old Testament prophecies. His birth and the events of his life had been foretold by many prophets during a period of 1,500 years.

Various prophets foretold of his miraculous birth, the place of his birth, his divine character, the purpose of his ministry, how he would die, and that he would be raised to life. These prophecies represent only a few of the many predictions made about Jesus's life, ministry, death, and resurrection. And he fulfilled every one down to the very last detail. History confirms beyond a doubt that Jesus is the true Messiah, the Son of God, and the Savior of the world.

GOD'S PLAN UNFOLDED IN THE PERSON OF CHRIST

The apostle Paul wrote:

> Blessed be the God and Father of our Lord Jesus Christ, who [God the Father] has blessed us in Christ with every spiritual blessing in the heavenly places, even as he [God the Father] chose us in him [Jesus] before the foundation of the world, that we should be holy and blameless before him [God the Father]. In love he [God the Father] predestined us for adoption as sons through Jesus Christ, according to the purpose of his will [God the Father], to the praise of his [God the Father] glorious grace, with which he [God the Father] has blessed us in the Beloved [Jesus]. In him we have redemption through his [Jesus] blood, the forgiveness of our trespasses, according to the riches of his grace, which he lavished upon us, in all wisdom and insight making known to us the mystery of his [God the Father] will, according to his [God the Father] purpose, which he [God the Father] set forth in Christ as a plan for the fullness of time, to unite all things in him [Jesus], things in heaven and things on earth.
>
> —Ephesians 1:3-10 (ESV)

The focus of these verses is what God the Father has done for us through the person of Jesus. These verses from Ephesians underscore the importance of Jesus' role in the adoption process. Don't read these words as the words of a theologian, but read them as a letter of love to a child who is greatly loved and sought after by a loving Father and Son.

In this first chapter of Ephesians, the focus of what God the Father has done for us is summed up in a person, his Son Jesus Christ. It was through his Son that we received God's love and grace.

It was an expensive endeavor. Our redemption and forgiveness came about through the giving of a life. Our adoption was a result of this great gift. It was the plan all along that this would be expressed through his only begotten Son, Jesus, and his giving himself for us ("to unite all things in him").

> This is good, and it is pleasing in the sight of God our Savior, who desires all people to be saved and to come to the knowledge of the truth. For there is one God, and there is one mediator between God and men, the man Christ Jesus, who gave himself as a ransom for all, which is the testimony given at the proper time.
>
> —1 Timothy 2:3-6 (ESV)

Jesus remains consistent with his Father's characteristics. He desires all men and women to be rescued and to experientially know the truth of who they are and what life is about. As we have seen, God the Father was willing to give his only begotten Son in order for us to have a relationship with him. We see in 1 Timothy that Jesus did this willingly. He "gave himself as a ransom" for us. The love the Father has for his children is shared by Christ.

THE NEW FAMILY VALUE OF FORGIVENESS

Through the sacrifice of our elder brother Jesus, you are forgiven. Meditate on that awhile. According to the New Testament, all your sins—past, present, and future—have been cast onto him, nailed to the cross, and died for.

> In him we have redemption through his [Jesus's] blood, the forgiveness of our trespasses, according to the riches of his grace, which he lavished upon us. . .
>
> —Ephesians 1:7-8 (ESV)

> There is therefore now no condemnation for those who are in Christ Jesus. For the law of the Spirit of life has set you free in Christ Jesus from the law of sin and death.
>
> —Romans 8:1-2 (ESV)

> For Christ also suffered once for sins, the righteous for the unrighteous, that he might bring us to God, being put to death in the flesh but made alive in the spirit.
>
> —1 Peter 3:18 (ESV)

YOU MAY GO, AND YOU MAY COME

As a result of what Jesus has done, you hopefully will experience a deep sense of forgiveness. In the next passage, Paul uses common language about Roman prisons at the time, called the "certificate of debt." In the day when this was written, a certificate of debt meant an itemized bond nailed to the prison door. It listed every crime for which the prisoner had been convicted. When the sentence was served or restitution paid, authorities removed the list and wrote,

"Paid in full." The prisoner used this as proof that he could never be tried for those crimes again. With this as background, now read these verses:

> When you were dead in your transgressions and the uncircumcision of your flesh, He made you alive together with Him, having forgiven us all our transgressions, having canceled out the certificate of debt consisting of decrees against us, which was hostile to us; and He has taken it out of the way, having nailed it to the cross.
>
> —Colossians 2:13 -14 (NASB 1995)

Use your imagination to picture what Paul wants you to see. He gives imagery in these verses of each of us as prisoners with a debt we cannot pay; above our prison doors are certificates of debt consisting of decrees against us. These decrees are a result of the crimes we have committed against the Holy God of the universe. On the certificate is also written the penalty for such crimes. According to the Bible, the penalty for the crimes we have committed against God is *death* (Romans 5:12 -21), not just physically but spiritually. Paul asks us to picture Jesus Christ going throughout the prison in which we are held captive, taking the certificates of debt from above our doors, unlocking our prison doors, then posting the certificates above his own head on the cross.

After such an act of love and forgiveness, can you imagine a believer choosing to remain in their prison cell? Christ has died and unlocked the door for the certificate of debt on the doorframe. He has declared the captive free from the penalty against him.

Remaining in the emotional prison cell of guilt and shame reveals what the believer actually believes about themselves and about what God has done.

At some point, this imagery from Paul should begin to move us emotionally in a very powerful, freeing way. If it does not, it may reveal a deep need and opportunity to explore why there is an absence of emotion about his forgiveness and love for us. We'll look at this more as we talk about our New Family.

LOVE, ACCEPTANCE, AND THE PERSON OF JESUS

> Long ago, at many times and in many ways, God spoke to our fathers by the prophets, but in these last days he has spoken to us by his Son, whom he appointed the heir of all things, through whom also he created the world. He [the Son] is the radiance of the glory of God [the Father] and the exact imprint of his nature, and he upholds the universe by the word of his power. After making purification for sins, he sat down at the right hand of the Majesty on high.
>
> —Hebrews 1:1-3 (ESV)

The implication of this passage in Hebrews is that we can actually observe the God of the Old and New Testament interacting with people on a daily basis through the person of Jesus Christ ("the exact imprint of his nature"). This is critically important to note.

Jesus stated it clearly:

> Jesus said to him, "Have I been with you so long, and you still do not know me, Philip? Whoever has seen me has seen the Father."
>
> —John 14:9 (ESV)

Jesus said he represented the full expression of God the Father. If we trust Christ and take him completely at his word, it means when a person interacted with Jesus, they were interacting with the God of the Universe.

"I and the Father are one."

—John 10:30 (ESV)

God the Son did not once say anything or behave in a way inconsistent with God the Father. Jesus represented the very nature of the Godhead.

Imagine God walking among us! What would it have been like to walk and talk with God? What kind of "vibe" would a person get hanging out with him?

Casual observation of the gospels reveals something striking in answer to these questions. The down and out, society's misfits, the unacceptable, the sick, the hurting, the poor, the "sinners," the undesirables, and the socially marginalized constantly flocked to Jesus. They were the ones dropping everything to follow him. They were the ones dropping to their knees in grateful worship and washing his feet with their tears and hair. If you knew nothing else about God, the facts about who felt comfortable around Jesus tell you everything about what God is like and what kind of vibe he gave to those around him. The unaccepted of Jesus' day obviously felt remarkably accepted by him.

The Son of Man came eating and drinking, and they say, 'Look at him! A glutton and a drunkard, a friend of tax collectors and sinners!'

—Matthew 11:19 (ESV)

And as he reclined at table in his house, many tax collectors and sinners were reclining with Jesus and his disciples, for there were many who followed him. And the scribes of the Pharisees, when they saw that he was eating with sinners and tax collectors, said to his disciples, "Why does he eat with tax collectors and sinners?"

—Mark 2:15-16 (ESV)

Now the tax collectors and sinners were all drawing near to hear him. And the Pharisees and the scribes grumbled, saying, "This man receives sinners and eats with them."

—Luke 15:1-2 (ESV)

In all probability, this meant that Jesus *verbally* and *nonverbally* communicated friendship, love, and acceptance on a continual basis to the "unacceptable" of his day. Think about it! For tax collectors and sinners to flock to him, he must have shown tremendous compassion, love, and understanding all over his face and in his body language. Everything he communicated nonverbally must have been very strong for the unacceptable people of that culture to feel comfortable continually approaching and drawing near him. Why? The social stigma that tax collectors and sinners had to overcome to hang around him is staggering.

- Jesus was considered a holy man and rabbi: it would be expected that only the "worthy" or "clean" could approach him.

- During the time of Christ, if you wanted to call someone a dirty name, you called them a tax collector.

- Tax collectors were rejected by their own culture as traitors and cheats.

- Tax collectors were considered the lowest of the low.

- Tax collectors were Jews who represented the Roman (non-Jewish) government, enforcing oppressive taxation on their own Jewish people.

The Pharisees and scribes were shocked and infuriated that Jesus befriended "sinners" and ate and drank with them. He clearly wined and dined with them frequently, because they accused him of being "a glutton and a drunkard." Why was observing Jesus sharing a meal with such people so infuriating to the Pharisees?

Eating and drinking with people during the time of Christ strongly communicated not just acceptance, but also commonality and friendship. You can bet the reason Jesus frequently ate and drank with the "unacceptable" was a strong intentional statement about himself. The Pharisees observed Jesus enjoying these people, acting in genuine friendship, and expressing real value to people labeled as rejects. By dining with them, Jesus communicated a strong nonverbal message to his observers: God loves those who have been deemed unlovable. This made many religious people uncomfortable, to say the least. They were scandalized by those with whom Jesus constantly affiliated.

Just as a great deal is revealed about Jesus through those who felt comfortable around him, much is revealed by those who felt uncomfortable around him. Jesus's interactions with those made uncomfortable by his behavior and words also tell you who he was and what he was about. Think about it: who felt uncomfortable around Jesus?

Jesus' contemporaries created a religious caste system of sorts. It was a system of being one step ahead or one step behind, in or out, acceptable or unacceptable. One dominant Jewish religious sect stated it plainly: "No madman, lunatic, simpleton, fool, blind man, maimed, lame, deaf man, or minor shall enter into the community." (Geza, 2012) Statements like these from religious leaders strongly communicated to people that God didn't want to have anything to do with the "unclean," the undesirables of their collective culture.

It was continually communicated verbally and nonverbally that you must meet certain standards to be acceptable to God and his people. There was a huge degree of oppression supported by the religious leaders of Jesus's day. But this was not from God. This type of oppression was from a self-centered, egotistical, self-righteous, self-serving, prideful, and religiously-confused people. Jesus's acts of love and acceptance for the "unrighteous" exposed the religious leaders for what they were—hypocrites. And they hated him for it.

The fact that religious leaders of Jesus's day despised and rejected him tells you *everything* about who he was and what he continually communicated to those around him.

THE SON OF GOD AND REJECTION

Jesus was well-acquainted with rejection. During his life on earth, he experienced more rejection than acceptance by the ones he dearly loved. He was rejected by his home town, his homeland, his people, and the religious leaders of the nation of the people he longed to provide for and protect. His heartache can be heard:

> "O Jerusalem, Jerusalem, the city that kills the prophets and stones those who are sent to it! How often would I have gathered your children together as a hen gathers her brood under her wings, and you were not willing!"
>
> —Matthew 23:37 (ESV)

- His own family questioned him.

- His closest friends betrayed him.

- His followers abandoned him.

- His countrymen traded his life for the life of a terrorist.

- Those he longed to draw close to showed the ultimate rejection by nailing him to a cross.

The prophet Isaiah stated it well:

> For he grew up before him like a young plant, and like a root out of dry ground; he [Christ] had no form or majesty that we should look at him, and no beauty that we should desire him. He was despised and rejected by men; a man of sorrows, and acquainted with grief; and as one from whom men hide their faces he was despised, and we esteemed him not.
>
> —Isaiah 53:2-3 (ESV)

Jesus knew all too well what it was to be disliked, despised, marginalized, unacceptable, and deemed an outcast. If there is anyone who can relate to the pain of rejection, it is our Savior, Jesus. With him, the issues of acceptance and rejection were *personal*.

JESUS'S LOVE IS PERSONAL

Most of us live with a haunting question: Am I worth knowing? Am I worth being chosen and invited into a significant, joy-filled relationship, especially by the Holy God of the universe? To be told or reminded that human beings in general are worth knowing, that we *all* qualify to be chosen as a group of people, does not help. The issue is this: Is the person you are inside worth knowing and lovable? It is exciting and somewhat comforting that "God so loved the world that he gave his only begotten Son," but the more pertinent questions in our hearts are these:

- Does God like me personally?

- Does he have intense feelings about me personally?

- Does he take joy and delight in me?

- Can God—who is holy, and whom we often fear, respect, admire, and worship—truly like me and feel passionate about knowing me as an individual?

- Would he have died for just me?

There are many who say, "Yes, undoubtedly. Jesus loves people and died for them; but his love and death on the cross were for the masses, for the world, not for me personally." Many Christians have the attitude that God has to save us because it's in his job description. Some Christians' concept of God's love for us is that it's solely an act of his will: he chooses to love us, holding his nose as he does so. Statements and beliefs like these arise through a skewed perspective of God and a misunderstanding of Scripture. Make no mistake about it: *Jesus, your elder brother and Lord, loves you personally! He would have died for you and you alone!*

JESUS NOTICED THE ONE IN THE CROWD

A quick glance through the gospels reveals a Savior who constantly pays special attention to individuals while surrounded by the masses.

In the book of Luke, Jesus answers questions like "But would he have done it for *me*?" with a series of stories, which are among the most famous in the Bible. These stories answer two questions:

- Does God like individual people?

- When individual people turn to God, is heaven happy about it?

In Luke 15:1-2, the Jewish religious leaders were complaining about Jesus's social habits of attending parties with tax collectors and sinners. In response, he tells them three short stories to illustrate how heaven works and why he does what he does.

THE LOST SHEEP

Jesus tells a story about just one lost sheep. A shepherd who had 100 sheep lost one of them. The shepherd left the other 99 behind and went after the one that was lost. After finding it, he placed it on his shoulder and while walking back, "he continually rejoiced." (Luke 15:5) The next verse tells us the shepherd threw a party with his friends and relatives, telling them to rejoice with him that he found his one lost sheep. Then Jesus said there was more joy in heaven over *one sinner's rescued life than over 99 in no need of rescue.*

THE LOST COIN

In the next story, a woman lost one silver coin out of 10. It may have been dowry money women sometimes sewed into their garments as a decoration and reminder of their marriage. The coin likely also had sentimental value. Jesus tells of the woman sweeping the floor of her house, lighting a lamp, and searching carefully for the coin. That single coin mattered deeply to her. When she found it, such joy overwhelmed her she threw a party to celebrate that single coin being found. Jesus again made the comment that there was more joy in the presence of the angels of God when one sinner turned to God.

THE LOST SON

The next story follows the same pattern. We see a desperately lost son (though later we'll discover there are actually two individually lost sons in the story, each lost in their own way). When the one wandering, prodigal son returns home, we see the father throw a party. Notice how the numbers change in the stories. They go from 100 in the first story, to 10 in the second, and down to two (sons) in the third. This is an intentional element of the storytelling, showing that in any group, of any size, the individual matters to God. He sees and he notices.

God intended these stories to explain heaven's value system to the Pharisees. Heaven values the individual! God throws heavenly parties over individuals.

Jesus explains why he attended sinner's parties and why he spent time with outsiders: he loved individual tax collectors and sinners. He ate and drank with them because he deeply delighted in them and was moved to go out of his way (like the people in the stories) to be with them individually.

Does God the Father feel the same way? Obviously! He represented the Father perfectly.

Jesus clearly states in these few stories (and there are more) that if you were the only person who was lost, he would go out of his way to find you, die for you, and throw a party in all of heaven—for you!

"But God, being rich in mercy, because of the great love with which he loved us, even when we were dead in our trespasses, made us alive together with Christ—by grace you have been saved— and raised us up with him and seated us with him in the heavenly places in Christ Jesus, so that in the coming ages he might show the immeasurable riches of his grace in kindness toward us in Christ Jesus."

—Ephesians 2:4-7 (ESV)

CHRIST'S LOVE IS OUR FOUNDATION

He does not deal with us according to our sins, nor repay us according to our iniquities. For as high as the heavens are above the earth, so great is his steadfast love toward those who fear him; as far as the east is from the west, so far does he remove our transgressions from us.

—Psalms 103:10-12 (ESV)

"For God so loved the world, that he gave his only Son, that whoever believes in him should not perish but have eternal life. For God did not send his Son into the world to condemn the world, but in order that the world might be saved through him."

—John 3:16-17 (ESV)

The sacrificial act of Jesus giving his own life in order for you to have life is the ultimate act of love. This great love revealed in Jesus Christ is to be the very foundation of our psyches. This is essential to our understanding to help us counter the negative effects of our fallen nature, fallen culture, and dysfunctional family backgrounds.

Paul encourages us to make these truths the very foundation of our inner lives. Review Paul's prayer for the believers in Ephesus:

> So that Christ may dwell in your hearts [the core of your beliefs, where you deeply feel about things you are thinking] through faith—that you, being rooted and grounded in love, may have strength to comprehend with all the saints what is the breadth and length and height and depth, and to know [experientially] the love of Christ that surpasses knowledge, [your previous experiences of what love is] that you may be filled with all the fullness of God.

> —Ephesians 3:17-19 (ESV)

Paul exhorts that the foundation of our spiritual and emotional lives is to be the love of Christ. He prays we will comprehend the full spectrum of this love.

At this point, we should consider what is actually the foundation of our Christian life? Have things other than Christ's love crept in and become foundational to our faith? It's an important question. Remember, our emotions are simply responding to what we deeply think and believe. It's possible that if we don't have the correct truth at the foundation of our Christian lives, we may be experiencing negative emotions as a result of believing something that is false. To see this, an illustration may be helpful.

As believers, we should go about our daily lives acting on facts, not living out of our emotions. Our emotions react to whatever facts we actively believe. However, as believers, we often do not run our lives on the facts of the most life-changing Scriptural truths.

We should focus not on what we need to do for him, but what he has done for us.

If our "facts" consist of the things we need to be doing as Christians, and if the things we do are the foundation of our Christianity, then our faith in those facts will have corresponding emotional results.

For example, the possible emotional response to the belief "I need to share the gospel more" may be that you feel pride because you did something for God. The "fact" you believe is that you need to perform, so the corresponding feelings may be pride or anxiety or shame. Or you may feel like a failure as a result of not doing anything for God.

But if you base your faith in the unchanging facts of what God has done for you through his Son, and his great love for you, your emotions will respond accordingly. Be very careful of the beliefs that pull your train!

Love is responsive in nature. Love is not generated out of thin air. If you were told, "You need to passionately love Harold," you would naturally ask me, "Who is Harold and why should I love him?" You would need more information about Harold so that you could respond by loving him. The nature of love is that it is responsive to something we see in a person or about a person.

Anyone who does not love does not know God, because God is love. In this the love of God was made manifest among us, that God sent his only Son into the world, so that we might live through him. In this is love, not that we have loved God but that he loved us and sent his Son to be the propitiation for our sins. Beloved, if God so loved us, we also ought to love one another.

—1 John 4:8-11 (ESV)

John is telling us something about the nature of love. To *know* God is to love him! The natural response to the person of Jesus Christ and what he has done for us is gratefulness and love. If I put my daily active trust in the fact that Christ loved me enough to die for me, and as a result I know I am totally forgiven, my emotional life will respond accordingly. I will feel deeply loved. My inner life will respond to that love. I will not only love him back, but according to this verse, I will love other brothers and sisters in Christ as well. If my inner life is not responding to God by loving him back, it is possible I believe the wrong facts about him. To know him is to love him.

A NEW SET OF COMPULSIONS DRIVING US

In an unhealthy family environment, family members develop compulsive behaviors as a result of inner turmoil caused by the dysfunctional family environment. In our New Family environment, there is a different set of compulsions. The apostle Paul says the love of Christ lays the foundation for a new set of inner compulsions:

For the love of Christ controls us, because we have concluded this: that one has died for all, therefore all have died; and he died for all, that those who live might no longer live for themselves but for him who for their sake died and was raised.

—2 Corinthians 5:14-15 (ESV)

The inner compulsions that drive and control us as children of God come from the family environment of knowing we are immensely loved and are of great worth. There is now a new set of instincts driving us as followers of Christ. The eldest Son of the family gave his life for the other family members. This now becomes a deeply emotional and powerful driving force within the family. It is no longer the pain of shame, guilt, and worthlessness that drives us; it is a tremendously powerful and memorable act of love and sacrifice that drives our inner lives.

WHAT IF YOU DON'T FEEL ANYTHING TOWARD GOD?

Many times, people do not *feel* anything concerning their relationship with God. As mentioned before, this can be due to being emotionally shut down because of cultural or family backgrounds. It is God's desire for his children to experience an emotionally rich family environment.

As a result of what Christ has done for us, our active trust in him would typically generate tremendous feelings of gratefulness, forgiveness, and love. If you are not experiencing these types of emotions from time to time at any level, it's likely one of the following is true:

- You actively believe the wrong facts concerning who God is and what he has done for you.

- You experience the results of being emotionally shut down from a dysfunctional background and are in need of having your heart resuscitated by a loving, Heavenly Family environment.

I cannot express strongly enough God's desire for you to feel and know his love and his heart. He sees you. He cares for you. He longs for you to live in and be compelled by his love and grace. I invite you to bravely practice leaning into the rich emotional life of your Heavenly Family—their arms are wide open, awaiting you.

QUESTIONS

Read Ephesians 1:3-10 again, taking note of words or sentences that are especially meaningful to you. Which words touch your emotions and give you comfort, hope, belief, and assurance? Which words communicate love to you and give you reason to trust God?

_____

_____

_____

_____

_____

In your own words, explain why it is important to realize that your salvation is not through a concept or a philosophy, but through a person?

_____

_____

_____

_____

_____

Imagine: what did Jesus communicate to those who felt unacceptable in their culture that was strong enough to overcome these powerful social barriers? Using your imagination, describe Jesus's nonverbals in his encounters with "tax collectors and sinners" in the gospels?

_____

_____

_____

_____

_____

IMMERSE YOURSELF IN GOD THE SON'S LOVE AND ACCEPTANCE

Jesus says:

- I am God the Son. (Luke 1:32)

- I am the Alpha and Omega, who is and who was, and who is to come. (Revelation 1:8)

- I am the only begotten Son of the Heavenly Father. (John 1:18)

- I have always existed with the Father and Holy Spirit. (John 17:22-24)

- I am the exact expression of God the Father's character and personality. (Colossians 1:15, Hebrews 1:3)

- I am the very expression of *truth* in the flesh. (John 1:14, 14:6)

- I am the summing up of God's redemptive plan, works, and business methods. (Ephesians 1:9-10)

- I am the revelation of God's mysterious plan for mankind. (Ephesians 3:2-6)

- I am the first born of the Heavenly Family. (Romans 8:29)

- I became flesh and walked, ate, drank, slept, laughed, cried, listened, rejoiced, and suffered just like you. (Hebrews 2:14, John 1:14)

- I am not religious, loading people down with heavy religious expectations. (Matthew 11:28)

- I am easy-going, relaxed, and refreshing to you. (Matthew 11:28-29)

- I am not pushy with people. I am humble at heart. (Matthew 11:30, Philippians 2:3-5)

- I am extremely patient. (1 Timothy 1:16, 2 Peter 3:9)

- I have an abundance of grace, active trust, and love. (1 Timothy 1:14)

- I am God's visible expression of his love and acceptance. (Matthew 11:19)

- Consider yourself *right now* seated between God the Father and myself in Heaven. (Ephesians 2:6)

- You are the ongoing, beautiful poem that I'm personally writing. (Ephesians 2:10)

- My love for you is deeper and more vast than you could ever imagine. (Ephesians 3:18-19)

- I want to give you life abundantly and cause your cup to overflow. (John 10:10)

- I willingly gave my life for *you*, with no feeling of obligation whatsoever. (Ephesians 5:2, Galatians 2:20)

- I gave my life as payment for your adoption into your new Heavenly Family. (Ephesians 1:5)

- My love for you far surpasses any previous experience you've had of love. (Ephesians 3:19)

- I want my love for you to be the foundation of all your thoughts and activities. (Ephesians 3:17-18)

- Let my steadfast love for you be your new obsession, controlling your thoughts and emotions. (2 Corinthians 5:14-15, 2 Thessalonians 3:5)

- Nothing will *ever* separate you from my love. (Romans 8:35-39)

CHAPTER 11

The Religiously Confused Home

We might assume that if a person grew up in a Christian home where Jesus Christ was daily lifted up as supremely important to the family's values, the home would naturally thrive, with healthy thinking and healthy emotions. It would be a home where Christ's loving-kindness and grace would be acknowledged during most meals together, along with words of gratefulness about God's unfailing provision for the family. Both the father and mother would be seen reading their Bibles on occasion, and even family devotions would be done on a weekly basis, at least when the kids were young.

Of course, they would rarely miss church on Sundays or mid-week Bible studies. The kids would be required to attend Sunday school, and as they grew older, required to attend youth group meetings. Dad may serve as a church leader and Mom as a leader on several committees or as the chairperson of the women's ministry committee.

Often in the home you would hear phrases like, "What would God think of you doing that?" or "Jimmy, what would Jesus do?" Clear statements of right and wrong would often be said, but not explained. The neighbor next door, known to be a divorced alcoholic, would often be lifted up to the children as an example of what not to be. Television viewing would be highly scrutinized along with what the children were viewing on the internet and in books and magazines, saying words like, "Would Jesus watch this?"

We might assume that this type of home would automatically be a healthy home, with a healthy view of God.

However, my experience tells a different story.

Imagine a home like the home described above, but the love and grace of God that were talked about were not actually felt among the family members. As a matter of fact, Mom and Dad were not all that happy. Regular displays of joy and laughter seemed to be oddly missing. This was odd to the children because their divorced alcoholic neighbor, whom their parents referred to as a poor role model, seemed genuinely happy. His laughter was real, along with his kindness toward the children.

When the parents did show emotion, it was usually anger and disappointment. It's not that the parents didn't smile, laugh, or be joyful at all, but the *majority* of the time, they were not happy. They frequently talked about the grace of God but seemed very performance-driven when it came to their relationship with each other and with the children. If the children behaved well, everything would be at peace; if they behaved poorly, swift and sure discipline occurred, along with emotional displays of anger. This was confusing to the children because when a child displayed anger, they were quickly disciplined for it.

Often the words "I love you" were said to the children, but said almost mechanically with very little warmth and affection. Sometimes they would pray and talk about lost people, those who didn't know Christ, but the children never saw the parents talk to people about Christ.

The parents regularly talked about their trust in God and how he always provided for their needs, but typically when the mom was paying the bills, she would cry, and there would be tension between the parents. The mom was often stressed or depressed. Sometimes when she was acting depressed, the kids would ask her if she was alright. She would appear to force a smile and say, "Yes dear, everything is fine. God is in control." Most of the time, the dad seemed oddly stoic and emotionally distant, preoccupied with work, and uninvolved with the family members. The exception to this was when he was called upon to discipline or correct the children.

These things were true until they arrived at church or church functions; then the parents would almost magically change. They would begin to smile and laugh and seem quite happy. The children began to realize this was what was normal for Christians. Even though there was pain and tension at home, you would smile and say everything was all right or just cover your emotions and say things like "God is good," when people at church ask how things are going.

This description paints a picture of the religiously confused home. It's a home that is involved with church and religious activities, but God's love and grace are *not deeply felt* and displayed among family members. Can you imagine how confusing it would be to children growing up in this home? Incredibly important biblical truths are read and talked about but they seemingly have no real effect on the home. God's love and grace are frequently referred to and lifted up as gifts, but love and grace are not practiced daily or displayed among the family members. Instead, rule- or law-keeping is experienced as the highest value. What seems to be the strongest value is not the person, but what the person does religiously. People from these homes are strongly confused because all the things that normally make a home healthy are talked about and lifted up with extreme importance, but a different instinctual behavior is being lived out in the home: instinctual behaviors that are driven by fear, guilt, and shame.

Imagine a home that uses shame, guilt, and fear as the main tools to shape behavior, a home where a child's performance is of supreme importance. You are imagining the religiously confused family's relational environment. This home environment typically produces three types of people. A child tends to either jump through the hoops and get with the religious program, rebel against the system, or lose his or her confidence due to the consistent reminder that he or she is not enough.

A Christ-filled home is different than the religious home.

In a Christ-filled home, the great truths of the Bible are not only talked about among family members, but they are instinctually lived out by the parents and deeply felt by the children in the home.

DIFFERENCES BETWEEN THE RELIGIOUSLY CONFUSED HOME AND THE CHRIST-FILLED HOME

Religiously Confused/ Dysfunctional Home	Christ-filled Home
God's love and grace are talked about but are not strongly felt among family members.	God's love and grace are not only talked about, but strongly felt.
Rule-keeping is the highest value.	People are of the highest value.
The Christian life is emphasized and lifted up to be of highest importance.	A personal relationship with God is emphasized and lifted up to be of highest importance.
What a person does is more important than who they are.	Who a person is, is more important than what they do.

Environment is heavy with unmet expectations.	Environment is one of peace and people feel free to be themselves.
Environment is unsafe and produces a "false self." The false self is lived out by parents.	Environment is safe and produces authenticity. Authenticity is lived out by parents.
Good behavior is of high priority.	Good character is of high priority.
Boundaries are established and maintained by rejection of behavior and of the person.	Boundaries are established and maintained by rejection of hurtful behavior, but *not* rejection of the person.
Displays of emotions are discouraged and not talked about.	Displays of non-manipulative emotions are encouraged and talked about.
Gratefulness for good behavior is most often expressed.	Gratefulness for people and how God has uniquely made each family member is most often expressed.
The Laws of God are lifted up and touted to be of highest importance.	People are lifted up and touted to be of highest importance. God's Law is taught, talked about, and actively trusted to be his way of protection and providence.
Doing the right things and being nice is strongly taught.	Right-doing and kindness is lived out by the parents and loving others like God loves is strongly taught and modeled by parents.
Parents are proud and self-centered. Authority and rules are overused to influence children.	Parents are broken and humble and use modeling, servanthood, and good communication to influence children.
Parents point out wrongdoing by others, but hide their own wrongdoing in order to appear righteous.	Parents are quick to apologize for their own wrongdoing and ask forgiveness from others in the family.

Make special note that the descriptions given are referring to the parent's beliefs, attitudes, and behavior—not the children's. The parents are the ones who must first actively believe and instinctually model healthy relationships and characteristics to their children. The children simply respond to what they see in their parents. This by no means guarantees the children will come out of the home being model citizens. It will, however, improve the chances they will not be confused about what a Christ-filled home is. The list describes general tendencies and is not meant to be exhaustive. The descriptions are not referring to what is talked about, but what is most strongly sensed or felt by the family members.

WHAT IF YOU ARE FROM A RELIGIOUSLY CONFUSED HOME?

It is important for the person who is from the religiously confused home to first realize in what ways their home was unhealthy. It is critically important for you to understand why your home experience was not what God intended for you. God intended parents of the Christ-filled home to personify God the Father's family characteristics. It is difficult for people from these homes to separate the great truths of the Bible from what they experienced in their family of origin.

Because religiously confused homes tend to be performance-oriented, it is crucial to remember not to add works of the Law to your faith in Christ. Adding obedience and works of the Law to the cross is like saying that the one-time act of the cross was not enough. God is most certainly aggrieved by our tendency to do this.

The Bible clearly teaches that Jesus's death on the cross was the greatest event in all of history. Christ himself said on the cross that with his sacrifice the payment for our sin was "finished." (John 19:28-30) It is the most important event in our New Family's history. Don't continue telling God, via your works and obedience to clear your conscience, that his Son's blood did not cover all your sin.

You must take time to sort out your family background and identify what was truly healthy and what was unhealthy. Take time to reflect on the fact that a Holy God who loves you gave his only Holy Son for you, without requiring anything from you in exchange. Because of the confusion caused by this type of religious home, it will take some real heart work and a lot of reflection to sort through these issues. It's incredibly valuable to have a trusted second party help you.

QUESTIONS

Can you relate to any of the religiously confused home descriptions? If so, how?

_____

_____

_____

_____

In your own words, describe the main difference between a Christ-filled home and a religiously confused home.

_____

_____

_____

_____

Do you live with a sense that even though Christ sacrificed his life for you, you must earn Jesus's forgiveness through obedience and works? If so, describe how it reveals itself in your daily life.

_____

_____

_____

_____

Is there anything else that struck you during this lesson that you believe God is inviting you to let him address?

_____

_____

_____

_____

CHAPTER 12

God the Holy Spirit and Our New Family Environment

THE HOLY SPIRIT AND OUR NEW FAMILY ENVIRONMENT

We are invited to join in a New Family, an everlasting, loving relationship with the family of the Trinity. This eternal family—God the Father, God the Son, and God the Holy Spirit—existed long before the creation of man.

According to the New Testament, each member of the Trinity is involved in our salvation and deliverance. The love and acceptance that exist among the Father, Son, and Holy Spirit are the basis of the love and acceptance that is shared with us.

The Father loves and actively pursues us.

The Son loves us and actively sacrifices for us.

The Spirit enlightens, teaches, empowers, and protects us.

Each of these are *persons*, not concepts. They are relational in the core nature of who they are. To approach the Trinity as a set of concepts is absolutely confusing and inaccurate. What each of them has done, are doing, and will do creates the present and future of our New Family atmosphere.

God the Father in the Trinity has never been an absent father. Instead of leaving us in our fallen condition, he made the ultimate sacrifice by giving us his innocent Son. Jesus, in his immeasurable love for us, willingly bore the pain and shame of the cross so that we could be adopted into the Family. The Holy Spirit, who indwells us, helps teach us these new spiritual realities and empowers us in our belief and active trust in our new Trinitarian Family.

Untold numbers of people have gone through wretched childhoods. Most have never effectively connected with others as an adult, so they have no reference for how horrible their pain was and is. Sadly, the pain is still normal in their adult lives; it is simply the atmosphere of their hearts.

Figuratively speaking, it's like having leprosy. People with physical leprosy have nerve damage that causes loss of feeling in their skin and muscles. Due to this lack of sensation, they can experience repeated, unfelt injuries; their toes, fingers, and limbs may decay and fall off, but they feel nothing. Something is wrong but they have no sensory perception of the loss. People with emotional leprosy experience pain so regularly in their hearts that they may no longer even call it pain—it's just home. They don't know that they have no context for the ability to feel genuine love, joy, trust, and peace. They simply cannot feel what's missing. That inability to feel causes them to miss the entire point of existence: connection and caring.

It's the great wound of abandonment. The need for belonging is in everyone, but for so many it gets submerged under painful wounds of neglect and disconnection.

These wounds leave the heart paralyzed and absent of feeling.

For the majority of people growing up in American homes, neglect and/or abandonment is the common experience within the family of origin. As I stated in earlier chapters, neglect is the most common form of abuse.

An example is when the words "I love you" are said, and the person saying it proceeds to nonverbally communicate things that negate those very words, such as ignoring or paying very little attention to the person they supposedly love. Or when a child hears "I love you" from a parent and those words are eventually followed by the parent announcing they are leaving because of divorce. The conclusion often drawn from these types of scenarios is, "Oh, I see. Critical family relationships end, love ends, promises are not fulfilled. These are empty words."

We conclude key relationships cannot be trusted or counted on. We believe if we get too close to someone, we are just setting ourselves up to be deeply hurt. Sadly, we then begin our own marriages and families with the same understanding and expectation of family life.

Unfortunately, we often enter our new Heavenly Family—and our relationships with people in the body of Christ—with the same understanding and expectations, too.

Hopefully, a child of God would have within them a deep sense of security because of their connection with the Trinitarian family. We have seen that God the Father communicates both verbally and nonverbally that we can trust him. He takes his relationship with us seriously. We were made in the image of the "relational ones." The Trinity is profoundly interconnected and our own desire for belonging goes all the way back to how we were created: we were designed to mimic the Trinity as relational ones.

We are made in the image of a person who has experienced infinite and unlimited connection. Being made in his image, you were created for *loving* connection. The greatest proof something is wrong in our part of the universe is that many of us have no sense of the terrible loss we suffered when the Fall occurred. Only three hours of separation from the Father on the cross drove Jesus to despair and profound questioning. He was so torn apart because of his deep connection with the persons of the Trinity. Oh, for our hearts to have such a connection with God, to intimately know and experience

God and his love in such a way that we would deeply mourn any disconnection from him!

The overflowing love from the Father is the answer to the pain of neglect and abandonment. God's love and affection for individuals reconnects our hearts to God and to one another. The ministry of the Holy Spirit is to make sure we are emotionally reconnected to the Father.

Paul the apostle assumed the normative Christian experience was an unforgettable experience of feeling loved by the Father. Many Christians do not seem to have experienced this; this is the main reason the *Untying the Knots of the Heart* process was developed. Hurting, broken hearts need to know how this emotional and relational connection can be obtained. We need to know this hope that does not disappoint us, as Paul talked about in Romans 5:

> And hope does not disappoint [putting us to shame], because the love [delighted passion] of God has been [permanently] poured out within our hearts through the Holy Spirit who was given to us.
>
> —Romans 5:5 (NASB 1995)

Paul uses the Greek perfect tense to describe this experience of being passionately delighted in us as individuals (otherwise known as Agape love). This perfect verb tense indicates that the love experience exploded with such force in the past that it is unforgettable, and its impact continues into the present. The Holy Spirit was the agent of the experience, but the experience was with God the Father. The one who willingly sacrificed himself for us was Jesus the Son. For many Christians, the Trinity is wholly mysterious instead of revered and understood. As we make the Father central, the Son and Holy Spirit naturally fall into their proper roles.

ARE YOU PART OF HIS FAMILY?

At this point, we'd like to encourage you to pause, examine your heart, and be honest with yourself. Do you sincerely know and have assurance that you are a part of God's Heavenly Family? Have you truly entered into life's most critical relationship? Have you placed your active trust in the person of Jesus Christ by expressing to God the most important Heavenly Family virtue, your belief and trust in him?

> But what does it say? "The word is near you, in your mouth and in your heart" (that is, the word of faith that we proclaim); because, if you confess with your mouth that Jesus is Lord and believe in your heart that God raised him from the dead, you will be saved. For with the heart one believes and is justified, and with the mouth one confesses and is saved. For the Scripture says, "Everyone who believes in him will not be put to shame." For there is no distinction between Jew and Greek; for the same Lord is Lord of all, bestowing his riches on all who call on him. For "everyone who calls on the name of the Lord will be saved."
>
> —Romans 10:8-13 (ESV)

This passage is clear: heartfelt belief, trust, and confession in Christ and what he has done for you results in your eternal salvation. If you call out to him, placing your faith in him and what he has done, you can *know* you are saved, a beloved child of God.

> But to all who did receive him, who believed in his name, he gave the right to become children of God.
>
> —John 1:12 (ESV)

You can have the greatest confidence and know without a doubt that you have eternal life and you are a child of God.

> And this is the testimony, that God gave us eternal life, and this life is in his Son. Whoever has the Son has life; whoever does not have the Son of God does not have life. I write these things to you who believe in the name of the Son of God that you may know that you have eternal life. And this is the confidence that we have toward him, that if we ask anything according to his will he hears us. And if we know that he hears us in whatever we ask, we know that we have the requests that we have asked of him.
>
> —1 John 5:11-15 (ESV)

The Bible tells us God loves you with a passionate, everlasting love. God satisfied his own nature, his own need for justice for mankind's sin and wrongdoing, by having his only begotten Son die on the cross and take the penalty of our sin onto himself. God's motive is clear: he wants to have a Father-son or Father-daughter relationship with you. He wants you to know him not just as your Savior and Lord, but also as your personal Father.

However, God is a true gentleman; he's not someone who will barge his way into your life. God desires that you enter into relationship with him through an active choice of your will. It's similar to a man and woman coming to the marriage altar, looking into each other's eyes, and taking one another as husband and wife. A man and a woman may enjoy each other and desire a relationship, but until they come to the altar and commit their hearts to one another, they are not yet husband and wife.

God is waiting at the altar of each person's heart, wooing, entreating, and calling out to come join him there. He is waiting for each of us to freely place our saving trust in him and what he has done to rescue us from eternal separation from him, drawing us to his heart.

> For all who are being led by the Spirit of God, these are sons of God. For you have not received a spirit of slavery leading to fear again, but you have received a spirit of adoption as sons by which we cry out, "Abba! Father!"
>
> —Romans 8:14-15 (NASB 1995)

According to the Bible, when we place our trust in Christ, his spirit testifies with our spirit that we are children of God. Does your spirit testify with his that you are a child of God?

Have you placed your active trust in Christ, asking him to be your personal Savior, expressing to him and others that he is Lord, in charge of not only this world, but also the next?

If you have already done this, you can have confidence you are his child, secure in his love. If you have not, I encourage you to go to the altar of your heart now to ask Christ into your life, receiving the gift of adoption as a child of God. Jesus said it only takes the faith of a mustard seed (a very tiny seed that grows into a huge plant) to move mountains and uproot enormous trees. Mountains and forests of sin between us and God can be removed and uprooted by faith the size of a mustard seed.

Participating in the Relational Environment of the Trinity

If you are a believer in Jesus Christ, you are a part of a New Family, a heavenly one. You are part of an everlasting love relationship with the Trinity!

It's often somewhat surprising, though, how believers in Christ know little about their New Family environment. I invite you to see Jesus' words in John chapters 14-17 as an invitation to an incredibly loving family; you will read words of committed, unwavering love and hope, words that stir your soul to trust each member of our New Family.

For many Christians, unfortunately, Trinitarianism is confusing at best. We don't quite know how we are to relate to this configuration, and such confusion does not result in blessings or comfort. We can also misunderstand the unique ministry of each of the persons of the Trinity, which leads to a boring and sometimes ignoble Christian life.

We want you to experience the great richness of the New Family values and their relational patterns. The Trinity is wonderfully unified in their activity, but differentiated in their involvement. Each member brings unique characteristics to this relationship. The Father is the focus person in the sense that we relate to him, and Jesus and the Holy Spirit sustain that relationship.

THE PERSON OF THE HOLY SPIRIT

We are in relationship with a triune God, a God made up of three distinct persons, yet self-declare themselves as one God. It's not that difficult to understand and imagine God the Father. Jesus seems even more tangible as a person that we can more easily grasp and relate to. But the third person of the Trinity, the Holy Spirit, is more mysterious and difficult to picture.

WHO IS THE HOLY SPIRIT?

The Holy Spirit is a person. Equal in every way with God the Father and God the Son, he is unquestionably considered the third member of the Godhead. All the divine attributes ascribed to the Father and the Son are equally ascribed to the Holy Spirit. The Holy Spirit is not some vague, impersonal force. The relationship of love and community that is shared among the three overflows into a relationship the triune God desires to have with every person. The Holy Spirit is an essential aspect of who God is. He is a person with all of the following:

- Intellect (1 Corinthians 2:11)

- Emotions (Romans 15:30)

- Mind (Romans 8:27)

- Will (1 Corinthians 12:11)

The Holy Spirit is referred to by multiple names:

- The Helper

- The Counselor

- The Advocate

- The Spirit of Truth

- The Holy Spirit

- The Holy Ghost

- The Spirit of Christ

- The Spirit of God

The word that is often translated *spirit* from Hebrew and Greek—the original languages of the Bible—also means *breath* or *wind*. In this image from nature, the Holy Spirit is like the wind—you can feel its effects when it blows, but you cannot see it.

Jesus said:

> "The wind blows where it wishes, and you hear its sound, but you do not know where it comes from or where it goes. So it is with everyone who is born of the Spirit."
>
> —John 3:8 (ESV)

Though the Holy Spirit may be more difficult to grasp as a person, the Bible gives us a few more tangible images we can easily imagine. One image for the Holy Spirit is that of an advocate or counselor.

When Jesus was teaching his disciples, he said:

> "These things I have spoken to you while I am still with you. But the Helper [Advocate, Counselor], the Holy Spirit, whom the Father will send in my name, he will teach you all things and bring to your remembrance all that I have said to you."
>
> —John 14:25-26 (ESV)

An advocate or counselor is a person who stands beside you, works with you, and supports your cause. The Holy Spirit is a counselor who supports, defends, teaches, and helps you in times of distress or trouble. This is the Holy Spirit's role for those of us who ask for his help in our lives.

During a small meeting with some Christian leaders, including myself, John Eldredge used humor to make an important point. He said something like, "Can you imagine your dad telling you that you are in serious need of a counselor? After declaring you have a great need for a counselor, he goes on to tell you he has taken the liberty to hire one for you. And not only has he hired one, he has asked the counselor to live with you, twenty-four hours a day, seven days a week, for the rest of your life." That is exactly what God the Father has done according to John 14:17.

In other passages, like Ephesians 1:13-14, we are told we are sealed with the promise of the Holy Spirit and given the guarantee of our inheritance as adopted children of God. In Romans 8:9-17, we are told many things concerning the Spirit of God. We're told that if we do not have the Holy Spirit in us, we are not actually children of God. But if we have the Holy Spirit within us, we can be led by the Spirit; the Spirit Himself will bear witness with our own spirits that we truly are children of God and as a result our souls will instinctually cry out, "Abba [Daddy, Papa]! Father!"

Through descriptions in John chapters 14-17, we learn many other things about the Holy Spirit and the critical role he plays in our lives:

- The Father sent the Holy Spirit.

- The world cannot behold or know him.

- He will reside in us.

- He will be in us forever.

- Jesus interchanges his own presence with the Holy Spirit.

- He will teach us all things.

- On the day he comes (which was the day of Pentecost), it will confirm that Jesus is in the Father and we are in him and he is in us.

- He bears witness of Jesus as the Christ.

- He will bring to remembrance all that Jesus said.

- He will testify about the Son.

- He will guide us in all truth.

- He does not speak on his own initiative; whatever he hears, he will speak to us.

- He will disclose what is to come.

- He takes whatever is of Christ and will disclose it to us.

The Word of God tells us the Holy Spirit also performs a role in the lives of non-Christians as well. He convicts people's hearts of God's truth concerning how sinful and broken we are—needing God's love and forgiveness, revealing who Jesus is and his death in our place for our sins, and God's eventual judgment of the world and those who do not know him (John 16:8-11). The Holy Spirit tugs on our hearts and minds, asking us to repent and turn to God for forgiveness and a new life.

AS A BELIEVER, CAN YOU IMAGINE LIFE WITHOUT THE HOLY SPIRIT?

For many of us the answer is yes, because we are unaware of the Holy Spirit's presence and ministry in our lives!

Important Biblical Truths About the Trinity, Our New Family:

- Only one God exists, yet he is expressed through three distinct persons (a deep, beautiful mystery).

- Any divine action always comes through a Trinitarian person.

- To speak of God acting is to speak of a member of the Trinity acting.

- Each Trinitarian member is fully divine but each member cannot be understood without reference to the other two.

- Every action is interdependent, but always done by a distinct Trinitarian person.

- The Trinitarian persons exist in an eternal love and sacred romance.

- Trinitarianism is Christianity.

- We discover the Trinitarian persons in the distinctions of their ministries or functions.

At this point, I want to make a careful distinction. Do not misunderstand that only the Father has love for us. Both the Father and Son have a personal love for us and it is shared in the person of the Holy Spirit. One of the distinct roles of the Holy Spirit is not drawing attention to himself; the Spirit expresses the love of the Father and Son, and draws us to them, to the family. In the passage below, the love of Christ and the love of the Father is expressed strongly along with words that provide confidence in our relationship with them.

> Who shall separate us from the love of Christ? Shall tribulation, or distress, or persecution, or famine, or nakedness, or danger, or sword? As it is written, "For your sake we are being killed all the day long; we are regarded as sheep to be slaughtered." No, in all these things we are more than conquerors through him who loved us. For I am sure that neither death nor life, nor angels nor rulers, nor things present nor things to come, nor powers, nor height nor depth, nor anything else in all creation, will be able to separate us from the love of God in Christ Jesus our Lord.

> —Romans 8:35-39 (ESV)

You can be sure nothing can separate the love of God from a child of God. He does not abandon his children. Note again that both the Father's love and the Son's love are mentioned; it is undeniably true we are loved by both, but the personal and relational element is directly attached to the Father, because he is the person of focus in the Trinity. The Holy Spirit expresses the presence and love of God the Father, and the foundation of the whole experience is what Christ has done for us.

There is a strong sense of security from the words in Romans 8:35-39. Those of us from a family of origin full of neglect and abandonment long to hear these words. But, because of our dysfunctional family backgrounds, these words are sadly met with suspicion and distrust. Our instincts to mistrust these comforting words emphasize our need to keep revisiting the cross, replacing false pictures of love and relationship with new pictures from our Heavenly Family.

More security in our relationships with God the Father is found in Hebrews:

> Keep your life free from love of money, and be content with what you have, for he has said, "I will never leave you nor forsake you." So we can confidently say, "The Lord is my helper; I will not fear; what can man do to me?"
>
> —Hebrews 13:5-6 (ESV)

This new certainty can lead us to freedom from things in our culture that bind or threaten us. The stock market can go up and down along with the rest of the economy, but for believers, their real futures and security are not in question.

Unfortunately, what happens so often is that new believers are run through the church experience so quickly, filled to the brim with all kinds of information at such blinding speed, that the next thing they know they are immobilized and sitting in a pile of jumbled information. Or so much is required of a new believer in terms of service expectations that they become immobilized as well. Instead, it would be best if believers were slowly walked through the new relationship they have with the Trinity so they can be grounded in the personal affection of the Father and his Son. It would be more beneficial if they were treated like a greenhouse rose, given lots of light, generous attention, and rich warmth.

WHAT IS A HEALTHY EMOTIONAL RESPONSE TO THE TRINITY'S LOVE?

Christians often appear like robots in their practice of Christianity. They appear to have no emotive response whatsoever to the affection the Trinity pours upon them. A robotic response can stem from believing they must win the Father's love by their actions. Frequently, emotionless Christianity drips from an exhausted heart that cannot believe it is loved.

What is at the heart of both of these reactions? A person may hear the truth of God's love, but real belief in it is trumped by background experiences. It could be ignorance, lack of biblical understanding, or beliefs in lies taught to them in the name of Christ—in other words, spiritual abuse.

The relationship God is calling us to is beyond our common understanding of true health. Sometimes we think spiritual health is supposed to feel like leprosy. Remember, with leprosy, a person loses physical feeling and sensation of any kind. As a result, their extremities are susceptible to injury and even being rubbed off because of their inability to sense pain.

Often in Christian circles we conduct ourselves like lepers; we keep moving forward in our Christian service feeling nothing and disintegrating before the eyes of a lost world. Being a Christ follower is not like that. God the Father desires us to feel the fullness of sensation and emotion. As we accept his Fatherhood by faith, allowing these realities to deeply penetrate us, such a relationship becomes possible.

Hopefully, God the Father's attention to our lives drives out the sense of abandonment grounded in our fallen families. If such things as the pigeons in the park and the number of the hairs on your head are a concern for the Father, then how much more your emotional life, relationships, and well-being must be a concern to him!

Some people leave a trail of disaster behind them, but God the Father leaves a trail of rich experiences. These experiences are critical. Without them, a viable and healthy Christian life does not exist. Every Christian benefits from the experience of being greatly loved and pursued by the Father. It is meant to be an absolutely normal part of our Christianity.

A CIRCLE OF LOVE

Finding a deep delight in each other, the Trinity wants to present one another in the best possible light. This was a matter of crucial concern between the Lord Jesus Christ and the Father. It's also what they desire from us.

> When Jesus had spoken these words, he lifted up his eyes to heaven, and said, "Father, the hour has come; glorify your Son that the Son may glorify you."
>
> —John 17:1 (ESV)

Invariably, the members of the Trinity glorify each other. The word glorify means to express or reveal the magnificent qualities of someone; to honor and extol the virtues of a person or thing; to lift them up and disclose the splendor of who and what they really are. In John 17, the Son asks the Father to help him present a correct and honorable picture of who the Father is so the Son can glorify him. That is a normal part of the love of the Trinity. The Father and the Son have a reciprocal loving relationship. Glorifying one another and loving each other is part of a reciprocal loving relationship.

In every truly healthy family, this type of reciprocal love is present. In the confused or dysfunctional home, usually one or both parents believes the other family members are there just to make them look good. It does not necessarily follow that the parents are there to love and glorify their children.

The Father and the Son desire to have a loving relationship with us. We were brought into the circle of love that predated the universe, and the love that existed then has now been shared with us.

> "The glory that you have given me I have given to them, that they may be one even as we are one, I in them and you in me, that they may become perfectly one, so that the world may know that you sent me and loved them even as you loved me."
>
> —John 17:22-23 (ESV)

> For you did not receive the spirit of slavery to fall back into fear, but you have received the Spirit of adoption as sons, by whom we cry, "Abba! Father!" The Spirit himself bears witness with our spirit that we are children of God,

and if children, then heirs—heirs of God and fellow heirs with Christ, provided we suffer with him in order that we may also be glorified with him.

—Romans 8:15-17 (ESV)

And one of the scribes came up and heard them disputing with one another, and seeing that he answered them well, asked him, "Which commandment is the most important of all?" Jesus answered, "The most important is, 'Hear, O Israel: The Lord our God, the Lord is one. And you shall love the Lord your God with all your heart and with all your soul and with all your mind and with all your strength.' The second is this: 'You shall love your neighbor as yourself.' There is no other commandment greater than these."

—Mark 12:28-31 (ESV)

The normal and healthy response to all God has done for us is tremendous amounts of gratitude and love toward him, lifting him up and glorifying who he is. The scribes and pharisees (the religious leaders during the time of Christ) could not love God with all their heart, soul, mind, and strength because they did not know him. They loved themselves and their religion. They generated their sense of honor and acceptance by being recognized for their adherence to the Laws of God; when Jesus gave them the greatest commandments of the Law, they could not fulfill them because they didn't know him.

HOW ABOUT YOU?

Are you responding to the love being extended to you in the New Family of the Trinity? If not, try to identify what is going on inside you and what you believe about God and his relationship with you. Talk about your experience with trusted individuals. Try your best to explain what you are feeling or not feeling. What facts do you actively believe (place your active faith in) to which your emotions are naturally responding?

What if you do not feel anything? Are you settling for leprous Christianity? Has your family background taught you to shut down your emotions, making you unable to fully enjoy the emotional benefits of your New Family in Christ? Are you disconnected from the reality of your new Trinitarian family's relational environment?

Remember, you were made in the image of God. You were created to be in loving connection with God the Father, the Son, and the Holy Spirit, and with other brothers and sisters of our New Family. Both the Father and Son have a personal love for you and it is shared in and through the person of the Holy Spirit. If you are a child of God you can be secure in the fact that nothing can separate you from his love and presence. Our Heavenly Father does not abandon his children! He leaves a trail of rich experiences behind him and these experiences are critical; without them, a viable and healthy Christian life does not exist.

QUESTIONS

Imagine life without the Holy Spirit. What would change in your life if you didn't have God's Spirit?

_____

_____

_____

_____

What do you think would characterize people who truly believe they are secure in God's love and that he would never forsake or abandon them?

_____

_____

_____

_____

_____

Do you ever fear God's abandonment? If so, how does that make itself evident in your life?

_____

_____

_____

_____

_____

How is your inner life responding to your New Family environment?

_____

_____

_____

_____

_____

CHAPTER 13

Taking Back Permission Slips

Most of us are unaware that we give others permission to tell us who we are and what we're worth. In other words we figuratively hand others permission slips to speak into our lives and define us.

Let me explain what I mean by permission slips. Imagine walking down the street and an older man who is a complete stranger stops you and says, "In case you were wondering what I think about you, let me tell you plainly. I think you are more worthless than a worm that crawls on the ground. As a matter of fact, I think the ground the worm crawls on is more valuable than you. You are lower than dirt in my eyes. I just thought you would like to know what I think of you." He then continues to walk on.

If this happened to you, would you listen to this man? Would you take his words about you to heart? Chances are you would not. Why? Because likely your answer would be "He doesn't know me, so I'm not going to listen to what he thinks about me."

But now imagine walking down the street and your father stops you and says, "In case you were wondering what I think about you, let me tell you plainly. I think you are more worthless than a worm that crawls on the ground. As a matter of fact, I think the ground the worm crawls on is more valuable than you. You are lower than dirt in my eyes. I just thought you would like to know what I think of you." He then continues to walk on.

If this happened to you, would you listen to him? Would you take your father's words about you to heart? Chances are you would, because he knows you, so you will give him permission to tell you who you are and what you're worth. In other words, you don't give the first man a permission slip to define you, but you do give the second man a permission slip to define you because he's your father.

Take a moment and write on a piece of paper three names of people whose voices you tend to listen to when you need and want to hear something positive about who you are and what you're worth. Those names could include your dad, mom, sibling, grandparent, aunt, uncle, friend, coach, teacher, etc. Then write down three names of people whose voices you tend to hear berate you and make you think and feel negative, hurtful thoughts about yourself. Again, the names may include family members, coaches, friends, peers, teachers, etc.

Imagine having six permission slips that say the following:

Permission Granted

Dear _____,

I give you permission to tell me who I am and what I'm worth! It is my intention to consider what you say and weigh it carefully along with the responses of others to whom I have handed these permission slips. I will then make a cumulative determination of who I am and what I am worth.

Signed _____

Warning: I may love or hate you based on your determination of who I am and what I'm worth. I will also count your nonverbal communication more heavily than your verbal communication. Please know that compliments will only be valued at 1/9 of the criticisms I receive from you.

Note the statement in small writing at the bottom of the slip.

Imagine writing each one of those names down that you listed on the paper, both the positive voices and the negative voices in your life, at the top of the slip and then signing your name at the bottom, giving them the right to tell you who you are and what you're worth.

What do you sense yourself feeling as you write their names on those permission slips? What does it feel like to give anyone the permission to define who you are and what you're worth? I would hope that you would feel a big knot in your stomach, and that it would feel awful, foolish, and wrong. Why? Because it is wrong! As a matter of fact, it's unbiblical!

According to the Bible, we are to only give God the permission slip to tell us who we are, what we're worth, and what life is about. We are *not* to give that permission slip to our parents, grandparents, siblings, spouses, children, friends, peers, coaches, teachers, bosses, or spiritual leaders. Not anyone! Why? Because how can someone who is still trying to figure out who they are be of any help to define you? It's the blind leading the blind.

As a Christian, I believe the only one who knows me and sees me clearly is God. He is the only one I trust to tell me who I am, what I'm worth, and what life is about. *God alone gets that permission slip!*

To be clear, there are other types of permission slips that can and should be appropriately handed to others. Like a permission slip (figuratively speaking) that says, "You can tell me how to do this skill," or "Instruct me how I can more wisely invest my money," or "Tell me which car or clothes dryer I should buy." These types of permission slips give others the right to speak into our lives in non-critical areas where the stakes are low. But in the areas that matter most—who we are, what we are worth, and where life is found—God is the *only one* who gets that permission slip.

So here are some important questions: To whom have you given these types of permission slips? Given this new perspective, to whom have you given permission slips you now need to take back? I believe these questions are critical to answer in your journey of recovery from your dysfunctional family as you move toward spiritual, emotional, and relational health.

A NEW WAY OF VIEWING OURSELVES

In the process of reparenting you, God the Father wants to paint a new picture across your heart of who you are. Do you believe that? It's true! If you have asked Jesus Christ to be your Savior and Lord, that process has already begun. You are in a New Family now. In this New Family, there are new values and new approaches God the Father wants you to employ. God the Father knows who you really are. Being a good Father, he wants to paint a picture across your heart of who you really are. To do that, your old perspectives and thoughts need to change.

If we are to be re-parented by God the Father, it is important to understand his family values and characteristics and for these to become an increasingly more natural part of our value systems. It's easy to say, but not simple to do. It requires a lot of reflection, meditation, heart work, and intentionality to make this transition. Reflection, meditation, and heart work are not important cultural values for many people. This will take real, concerted effort.

According to the Bible, our self-perception is meant to be based on how God the Father perceives us. Long before psychologists ever thought of the idea of self-image, the New Testament had already addressed the issue. God is calling you to a beautiful new way of viewing yourself and your life.

As we let go of our old views of self and life, embracing our new identities, a powerful dynamic happens within us. In the New Testament, the image we are meant to have of ourselves is God's view of us after we accept Jesus Christ as Savior. It is not based on nationality, social or economic standing, physical appearance, or gender. Take a look at the perspective given in Galatians:

> For in Christ Jesus you are all sons of God, through faith. For as many of you as were baptized into Christ have put on Christ. There is neither Jew nor Greek, there is neither slave nor free, there is no male and female, for you are all one in Christ Jesus. And if you are Christ's, then you are Abraham's offspring, heirs according to promise.
>
> —Galatians 3:26-29 (ESV)

God has provided a new way of thinking about and seeing ourselves through our New Family. We have been given a New Family heritage. Immediately following this description of how we have been immersed into Christ is a depiction of the psychological relationship we have as heirs of God. Our old families of origin and culture had a tremendous impact on each of us; the New Family should have an even greater impact.

We have a choice to make. We can spend the rest of our lives being defined by what was wrong with our family of origin and culture, or we can pursue our New Family as we sort out the baggage of our backgrounds.

One of the real problems with those who begin an archeological dig into their family background is that they may not be able to handle what they find there. They often have no helpful resources to deal with what they discover. They are defenseless, except to look to someone else who now has to be a substitute father or mother. We have a strong need to emotionally identify more with our New Family than with our old family of origin or culture. Tremendous spiritual power and resources will be unleashed as we do this. Look at the perspective God gives us:

> What shall we say then? Are we to continue in sin that grace may abound? By no means! How can we who died to sin still live in it? Do you not know that all of us who have been baptized into Christ Jesus were baptized into his death? We were buried therefore with him by baptism into death, in order that, just as Christ was raised from the dead by the glory of the Father, we too might walk in newness of life.
>
> —Romans 6:1-4 (ESV)

Paul reasons that what should keep a person from being passive or rebellious against God is their deep identification with the person of Christ and his death. Paul reasons that to walk in newness of life, you must picture your old self—your old identity and old approach to life and others—as crucified and buried with Christ. Just as importantly, you are to picture a *new self* raised with Christ in his resurrection. This call to identify with Christ is found throughout the New Testament.

OUR IDENTIFICATION WITH JESUS CHRIST

The works, character, and reputation of Jesus Christ are the keys to your new identity. In Romans 6:1-4, Paul says that according to

God we have been immersed into the person and works of Christ. Our identities with Christ mean we are permanently clothed with his achievements. Paul tells us that through a personal knowledge of this reality, we can break the power of negative moods, desires to hurt ourselves and others, and our enslavement to obsessive and compulsive drives.

Notice the phrase "Do you not know?" Paul says we break the cycle by knowing that we have a new identification, a new identity. From a Scriptural perspective, it is the old self-identities from our dysfunctional backgrounds that keep us enslaved. God the Father tells us throughout the New Testament that this new self-perception will help us to break free from guilt, sin, shame, desire, temptation, and wrongdoing.

As believers in Christ we are given value, esteem, and dignity, but unlike our old families, these things are not earned or deserved. They are given as gifts. In our New Family in Christ, God gives good gifts because of his character, not ours. In Christ, when God the Father looks at you, he thinks of his Son. When he looks at his Son, he thinks of you. God the Father is calling you and me to deeply identify with his Son and the greatest act of our New Family's history where it all began, the death and resurrection of Jesus.

God wants you to deeply immerse yourself with his Son. He wants you to emotionally sense the impact of his Son's great sacrifice on the cross, his death, and his resurrection. This is why you can let go of fallen, inaccurate views from your family of origin and your old identity. They cannot come close to God the Father and God the Son's acts of love and kindness toward you. What a relationship! What a heritage! If you deeply embrace this reality alone, it will result in the deep emotional response of gratefulness and love.

Right now, try to imagine and comprehend Christ's death on the cross for your sin. In this state of mind and emotion, would it be your desire to rebel against God your Father and to hurt someone else he loves? I would imagine not! Do you see the power of this type of perspective and thinking? You are seeing and feeling the psychological effect of this relationship and your New Family's relational environment.

If you are like me and come from a dysfunctional family background, you and I need to be intentional about the pictures and perceptions of who we believe we are.

> Do not eat the bread of a selfish man, Or desire his delicacies; For as he thinks within himself, so he is. He says to you, "Eat and drink!" But his heart is not with you.
>
> —Proverbs 23:6-7 (NASB 1995)

Solomon shares an important aspect of human nature: in modern language, he is saying we are not to be like someone driven by their inner compulsions (compelled by their view of themselves), preoccupying or medicating themselves. For such a person, their heart—their inner life—is all about themselves and their desires, not about anyone else. Solomon observes that a man's thoughts about himself ultimately affect his outward behavior: the picture you have within yourself of who you are, what you are worth, and what life is about is a powerful force.

It is important to get in touch with the past pictures of yourself in order to fully remove them and embrace God the Father's new pictures. It is necessary to examine ourselves and how we are processing these new truths in light of what we once believed about ourselves and about life—or Christianity will just be a surface exercise in platitudes and abstractions that makes no real impact on our lives. The gospel's sharp, iron edge will be reduced to the mushiness of oatmeal.

The apostle Paul says in his letter to the Ephesians that there is a distinction between learning truths and concepts and actually integrating those truths into our lives in a way that changes us. He says there must be an active laying aside of the old self and an active putting on of the new self.

> But that is not the way you learned Christ!—assuming that you have heard about him and were taught in him, as the truth is in Jesus, to put off your old self, which belongs to your former manner of life and is corrupt through deceitful desires, [the strong desire to hide and deceive ourselves and others about who we really are] and to be renewed in the spirit of your minds, and to put on the new self, created after the likeness of God in true righteousness and holiness.
>
> —Ephesians 4:20-24 (ESV)

Paul assumes we need to come to terms with our pasts and the patterns of our old selves in order to embrace the new truths of the present. He tells us to take off our old identities so we can put on the new ones. Common sense tells us that to take something off, we must know what that something is. So it's worth our time and reflection to understand our old selves—our old identities and ways of seeing the world—so we can truly begin to unload all they have done in our lives. Paul uses similar wording in his letter to the church in Colossae:

But now you must put them all away: anger, wrath, malice, slander, and obscene talk from your mouth. Do not lie to one another, seeing that you have put off the old self with its practices and have put on the new self, which is being renewed in knowledge after the image of its creator. Here there is not Greek and Jew, circumcised and uncircumcised, barbarian, Scythian, slave, free; but Christ is all, and in all.

—Colossians 3:8-11 (ESV)

Paul wanted the Colossians to recognize the concrete things they used to practice that result from their previous spiritual nature, family, and cultural backgrounds outside of Christ. An effective way a person can start meaningfully laying aside these unhealthy practices and identities is to compare and contrast what they have previously experienced with what God's New Family environment is like. This comparison and contrast will make clear our unhealthy practices, like trying to earn love, substituting a lower level of suspicion for true faith (active trust), and isolating during pain—as opposed to sorting things out in relationship where true affection, compassion, and comfort are found.

RENEWED IN THE SPIRIT OF YOUR MIND

Recovering from a dysfunctional family background will require you to renew your patterns of thinking and believing. This "putting on" that Paul talks about in Colossians 3 demands a total change of thought patterns. After Paul said to put off the old identity like soiled clothing, he said to "be continually renewed in the spirit of your mind."

God intends our minds to be made completely new; he wants to change everything in our old patterns of thinking. As we identify what we are "wearing" from the past, we are to put it away like soiled clothing and embrace a completely new set of clothes. We are to put on our new identities in Christ and a new set of daily practices.

> Put to death therefore what is earthly in you: sexual immorality, impurity, passion, evil desire, and covetousness, which is idolatry. On account of these the wrath of God is coming. In these you too once walked, when you were living in them. But now you must put them all away: anger, wrath, malice, slander, and obscene talk from your mouth. Do not lie to one another, seeing that you have put off the old self with its practices and have put on the new self, which is being renewed in knowledge after the image of its creator. Here there is not Greek and Jew, circumcised and uncircumcised, barbarian, Scythian, slave, free; but Christ is all, and in all.
>
> —Colossians 3:5-11 (ESV)

Do you see Paul's pattern as he talks about transformation and renewal? He commonly uses words and images of dying to something, taking something off, putting something aside, and then putting on something else. But the common key to the whole process of transformation is the renewing of the mind. God wants to renew our minds so we share his perspectives and thinking.

In this book we have begun identifying the lies or false beliefs to which we tend to cling from our dysfunctional family backgrounds, which in turn produce a cascade of painful emotions. To be transformed, we now begin replacing those lies with the truth of who we are, what we are worth, and what life is really about. This is the process of renewing the mind.

INTEGRATING GOD'S TRUTH INTO YOUR CONSCIOUS AND SUBCONSCIOUS MIND

God has a new set of pictures for the believer to embrace, which will create a thoroughly new way of thinking, feeling, and relating. Why is it that sometimes the truth—good, solid, biblical truth, which believers have heard hundreds of times—has not changed them? It is the crucial difference between information memorization and integration.

With information memorization, the conscious mind has simply placed it as data in the memory at best. With integration, the conscious mind has taken a picture formed in the imagination, reflected and meditated on it, and not just considered it as data, but has placed it in both the conscious and subconscious part of the mind, where it will affect the emotions.

Integration occurs as a child, when we intuitively look to others around us to tell us who we are and what we are worth. Children eagerly listen to both verbal and nonverbal communication from their parents, siblings, and peers, and others. They don't take it in as casual data, but with very childlike trust, place it in their subconscious where it affects their emotions and likely continues to affect them into adulthood.

When it comes to embracing your new identity and life in Christ, it's vitally important that you use integration as your mode of operation, as opposed to the casual, information-gathering we are susceptible to in our fast-paced, surface-level culture.

How Do We Integrate Truth?

The Bible uses some powerful concepts to put us into a truth integration mode, as opposed to just an information-gathering mode.

God tells us to consider our old selves as dead. The word "death" is an emotive word. Intuitively, if your life is on the line, you are immediately put into a truth-integration mindset. God also uses the imagery or picture of us becoming like children again in our approach to ourselves and the Kingdom of God.

Several Bible passages speak of us approaching God as a child or newborn:

> But Jesus called them to him, saying, "Let the children come to me, and do not hinder them, for to such belongs the kingdom of God. Truly, I say to you, whoever does not receive the kingdom of God like a child shall not enter it."
>
> **—Luke 18:16-17 (ESV)**

> Jesus answered him, "Truly, truly, I say to you, unless one is born again he cannot see the kingdom of God." Nicodemus said to him, "How can a man be born when he is old? Can he enter a second time into his mother's womb and be born?" Jesus answered, "Truly, truly, I say to you, unless one is born of water and the Spirit, he cannot enter the kingdom of God. That which is born of the flesh is flesh, and that which is born of the Spirit is spirit. Do not marvel that I said to you, 'You must be born again.'"
>
> **—John 3:3-7 (ESV)**

> Blessed be the God and Father of our Lord Jesus Christ! According to his great mercy, he has caused us to be born again to a living hope through the resurrection of Jesus Christ from the dead, to an inheritance that is imperish-able, undefiled, and unfading, kept in heaven for you,

who by God's power are being guarded through faith for a salvation ready to be revealed in the last time.

—1 Peter 1:3-5 (ESV)

Having purified your souls by your obedience to the truth for a sincere brotherly love, love one another earnestly from a pure heart, since you have been born again, not of perishable seed but of imperishable, through the living and abiding word of God.

—1 Peter 1:22-23 (ESV)

These pictures of becoming like children and being born again are powerful. Considering yourself as a child in your approach to God as your Father puts you into an integrative mindset. Children are like soft clay, easily shaped and molded. They have not been hardened by broken promises and relational pain. Children trust and place themselves willingly into the care of their parents and others.

In no uncertain terms, God is calling you once again to have a childlike trust in him alone, to approach your relationship with him as a child who desperately wants and needs your Father to tell you who you are and what you are worth.

Again, this is going to take intentional reflection, meditation, and heart work. You are not alone in this process. God promises that the Holy Spirit is there to help you. Actively trust God, and ask him through prayer to help you in the process of integrating his truths into your heart. Consider inviting a trusted person who would like to grow in these same ways to join you in the journey of practicing and integrating new perspectives.

It is vitally important to integrate the truths of who we are in Christ and what we are worth to God into the deepest parts of our psyches. We are not just doing the same old casual information gathering. We are truly renewing our minds and integrating his life-changing perspectives into our daily lives. We are resolving to die to our old selves, putting the old self off like a piece of soiled clothing and becoming like a child again, receiving and embracing our new identities and lives in Christ in full assurance and trust.

Participation in a community that promotes integration of these truths is vital to taking them into your own psyche. As you live in a new environment where these truths are talked about and lived out among your friends and family, you will begin to experience the positive emotional effects in your daily life and begin the process of recovering from your dysfunctional family background.

QUESTIONS

How do you think your life would be different if you did not define yourself by what others think of you?

_____

_____

_____

_____

With a new perspective about identity, to whom have you given permission slips that you now need to take back?

_____

_____

_____

_____

What would you do if someone gave you such a permission slip? Whose permission slip(s) are you currently holding? What should you do with these slips?

_____

_____

_____

_____

What might your life look like if God was the only one to whom you handed a permission slip to tell you who you are and what you are worth?

_____

_____

_____

_____

IMMERSE YOURSELF IN THE TRUTH OF WHO GOD SAYS YOU ARE

- I'm a greatly loved son/daughter of the almighty God, King of the Universe. (John 1:12, Romans 8:16, Ephesians 3:17–19, Romans 5:8)
- I'm a co-heir with Christ, sharing with him a great inheritance that is beyond imagination. (Romans 8:16–17, Titus 3:5–7, James 2:5)
- I'm a dwelling place of the Holy God of Israel. (1 Corinthians 6:19, John 14:16–20, Romans 8:10–11)
- I'm of unimaginable worth: I'm worth the suffering and death of the Holy Son of God. (Romans 5:6–8, John 3:16)
- I'm of an entirely different nature than before: eternally and spiritually alive. (2 Corinthians 5:17, 1 John 5:11–13)
- I'm a unique and valued family member of the great Trinitarian Family. (1 Corinthians 12:12–27, Romans 12:5–6, Ephesians 2:19–22)
- My gender uniquely expresses important characteristics of God. (Genesis 1:26–27)
- I'm adopted as a mature, fully-trusted son/daughter of God. (Galatians 4:1–6, Ephesians 1:5)
- I'm a steward of the Gospel of Christ and the great gifts given to me by the Father of Lights. (1 Corinthians 4:1–2 1, Thessalonians 2:4, 2 Timothy 1:14, 1 Corinthians 12:12–27, James 1:17)
- I'm an ongoing poem (work of art) that God is writing. (Ephesians 2:10)
- I'm an alien of this world; this is not my home. I'm temporarily passing through. (Ephesians 2:19, Philippians 3:19–21, 2 Corinthians 5:6–8, 1 John 3:1, John 17:13–14)

- I'm a "forgiven one," completely redeemed by a loving Father. (Colossians 2:13–14, Isaiah 43:25, 1 John 1:7, Ephesians 4:32)
- I'm a privileged co-sufferer with Christ in a fallen, sin-filled, and lost world. (Philippians 1:29–30, Romans 8:17, Matthew 5:10–11, Acts 5:41)
- I'm completely saved. I'm absolutely forever secure in his unchanging love. (1 John 5:11–13, Hebrews 13:5–6, John 10:28–29)
- I'm no longer alone or an orphan, but embraced by my New Family forever. (John 14:18, John 14:1–3, Matthew 5:25–30, Hebrews 13:5–6)

Acknowledgments

The book you are holding in your hands would not exist if it wasn't for the enormous efforts of Kathie Slusser Carlson. Kathie's wise contributions, intimate knowledge of the subject matter, and careful editing have been pivotal in taking this book to a higher level. Thank you, Kathie, for all that you have done to make this book possible.

Also, I will be forever grateful for Dr. David Eckman. God used Dr. Eckman in my life in a powerful way. David, it was because of you that I learned so much about how the Bible addresses family backgrounds. More importantly, it was because of you that the gospel went to where it was always intended to go: the deepest parts of my heart. Readers, I encourage you to go to Dr. Eckman's ministry website, BecomingWhatGodIntended.com.

I would also like to thank the following people. I could not have done this without their prayer, dedication, wisdom, sacrifice, diligent work, support, and friendship: Renee Rule, my children and grandchildren, Clancy Johnston, Kelly Damm, and Larry Cupp.

In His life-changing love and grace,

Tim Rule
Founder and Executive Director, InnerLife Ministries

About the Author

Tim Rule is the Executive Director of InnerLife Ministries, as well as the author and developer of the discipleship process *Untying the Knots of the Heart*. After graduating with a Bachelor of Science in Psychology from Idaho State University, Tim and his wife, Renee, joined the full-time staff of Campus Crusade for Christ (now Cru). They were on staff with Campus Crusade for over 26 years, the majority of those years serving as local and regional directors in California and the Greater Northwest college campus ministry.

Tim has over 40 years of experience in counseling and discipling Christians of all ages and is well known for his ability to help others sort through relational, emotional, and spiritual pain and difficulties using life-giving Biblical approaches. He is also a popular conference and retreat speaker both in the U.S. and abroad. His driving passion is seeing God bring true life change to people as they begin to grasp the realities of who they are to God the Father as well as the depth of His grace, forgiveness, and love. Tim and Renee live in Boise, Idaho. He is the father of four children and grandfather to a growing number of grandchildren.

About InnerLife Ministries

InnerLife Ministries exists to bring the gospel to the darkest places of the heart. Founded in 2009, InnerLife Ministries was created after director and founder Tim Rule found himself heartbroken over the fact that for so many Christians, something other than the gospel was having a bigger effect on their day-to-day lives and relationships. He knew it shouldn't be this way. Driven by this certainty, he founded InnerLife Ministries to help others experience the true and lifelong change of the gospel.

For over 12 years, InnerLife Ministries has effectively equipped leaders and churches worldwide to foster environments of transformative change in the life of the believer. Through their small group curriculum, *Untying the Knots of the Heart,* they have helped thousands address the root causes of heartache and relational problems by examining how spiritual, cultural, and family backgrounds can shape one's view of God the Father and one's self. *Untying the Knots of the Heart* has also allowed untold numbers of people to experience the redemption of their identity, pain, and emotions through the gospel of Jesus Christ.

Connect

If you have enjoyed this book and would like to go deeper, you would love the small group curriculum and process called *Untying the Knots of the Heart*.

We all experience pain and brokenness at different times in our life. Typically we respond by trying to change our behavior or circumstances without addressing the root causes.

Untying the Knots of the Heart brings the concepts in this book to life along with new concepts. It's a proven, life-transforming small group process that God uses to address the root causes of Christians' struggles and heartache. *Untying the Knots of the Heart* is so much more than a band-aid fix. It's truly life-transforming.

To learn more or find a group, visit UntyingTheKnots.org

Sources

Bradshaw, John. Bradshaw On: *The Family: A New Way of Creating Solid Self-Esteem*. Simon and Schuster, 2010.

Buechner, Frederick. *The Sacred Journey*. HarperCollins Publishers, 1982.

Felitti, V. J., Anda, R. F., Nordenberg, D., Williamson, D. F., Spitz, A. M., Edwards, V., Koss, M. P., & Marks, J. S. "Relationship of childhood abuse and household dysfunction to many of the leading causes of death in adults: The Adverse Childhood Experiences (ACE) Study." *American Journal of Preventive Medicine*, 1998. https://doi.org/10.1016/S0749-3797(98)00017-8

Gold, Jason; Wolan Sullivan, Margaret; and Lewis, Michael. The relation between abuse and violent delinquency: The conversion of shame to blame in juvenile offenders. *Child Abuse & Neglect*, 2011. https://pubmed.ncbi.nlm.nih.gov/21783253/

Hall, M., & Hall, J. "The long-term effects of childhood sexual abuse: Counseling implications." 2011. http://counselingoutfitters.com/vistas/vistas11/Article_19.pdf

Hemfelt, Robert; Minirth, Franck; and Meier, Paul. *Love Is a Choice: Recovery for Codependent Relationships*. Thomas Nelson Publishers, 1989.

Hymowitz, Kay; Carroll, Jason S.; Wilcox, W. Bradford; and Kaye, Kelleen, "Knot Yet: The Benefits and Costs of Delayed Marriage in America." *Faculty Publications*, 2013. https://scholarsarchive.byu.edu/facpub/4325/

Jacobson, Wayne. *He Loves Me!: Learning to Live in the Father's Affection* (Windblown Media, 2007), pp.18-19.

Lieberman, M. D. *Social: Why Our Brains Are Wired to Connect.* Crown Publishers/Random House, 2013.

Lynch John; McNicol, Bruce; and Thrall, Bill. *The Cure: What If God Isn't Who You Think He Is and Neither Are You?* (CrossSection, 2011), p.44.

McCain, John S. John McCain, *Prisoner of War: A First-Person Account.* (This story originally appeared in the May 14, 1973, issue of U.S. News & World Report. It was posted online on January 28, 2008.) https://www.usnews.com/news/articles/2008/01/28/john-mccain-prisoner-of-war-a-first-person-account

Strong, James. *New Strong's Exhaustive Concordance of the Bible.* Thomas Nelson, 1984.

Thompson, Curt. *Anatomy of the Soul: Surprising Connections between Neuroscience and Spiritual Practices That Can Transform Your Life and Relationships.* Tyndale/SaltRiver, 2010.

Wuest, Kenneth. *The New Testament: An Expanded Translation.* Wm. B. Eerdmans Publishing Co., 1961.

Vermes, Geza. *The Complete Dead Sea Scrolls in English.* Penguin Random House, 2012.

Made in the USA
Monee, IL
09 September 2021